W9-CDG-961

THIS LAND IS OUR LAND

THIS LAND
IS OUR LAND

HOW TO END THE WAR ON PRIVATE PROPERTY

Congressman Richard Pombo
and Joseph Farah

St. Martin's Press ✳ New York

THIS LAND IS OUR LAND. Copyright © 1996 by Richard Pombo and Joseph
Farah. All rights reserved. Printed in the United States of America. No
part of this book may be used or reproduced in any manner whatsoever
without written permission except in the case of brief quotations em-
bodied in critical articles or reviews. For information, address St. Martin's Press, 175 Fifth Avenue, New York, N.Y. 10010.

Production Editor: David Stanford Burr

Book design by Scott Levine

Library of Congress Cataloging-in-Publication Data

Pombo, Richard.
    This land is our land : how to end the war on private property /
by Richard Pombo and Joseph Farah.
        p.   cm.
    ISBN 0-312-14747-3
    1. Property, Right of—United States—Popular works.
    2. Environmental law—United States—Popular works.
    3. Environmental policy—United States—Popular works.   I. Farah,
Joseph.   II. Title.
    KF562.P66   1996
    346.7304'4—dc20
    [347.30644]   96-20254
                                                                  CIP

First Edition: September 1996

10   9   8   7   6   5   4   3   2   1

CONTENTS

ACKNOWLEDGMENTS

First I would like to thank my wife, Annette, and my children, Richie and Rena. When I first ran for office, it was out of fear my children would not have the same opportunities that I had been given by my father, and him by his.

I often wonder if the public life that we lead is worth it. But when I look into the eyes of my children, I know it is something that must be done.

My parents, Ralph and Onita, have been the greatest influence on my beliefs—both politically and spiritually. They raised five boys the best way they knew how, with the hope that they would grow to respect the values they hold so dear: God, family, and country.

Joe Gughemetti, an attorney, taught me that in the battle over property rights, it's not enough to be right. You also have to win.

I would like to thank the thousands of people who give of themselves to the private property groups not for themselves, but for their children and grandchildren. They understand that if we lose this battle today, we may never regain our constitutionally guaranteed rights.

A special thank-you must be given to Leroy Ornellas, Tony Souza, Jim Edwards, and Nanette Martin, who, with me, started the

San Joaquin County Citizens Land Alliance. Their help and support has made much of our progress possible.

To all the people who helped me gather information for this book, thank you, for private property is the backbone of the capitalist system and the lifeblood of free enterprise. Our Founding Fathers knew that, which is why they included the following in the Fifth Amendment of the Bill of Rights: ". . . nor shall private property be taken for public use without just compensation."

—RICHARD POMBO
Tracy, California

Thanks to Mike Antonucci, a gifted journalist and masterful researcher, who devoted several months to this project and provided the guiding force behind *This Land Is Our Land*. This book could not have been completed without his vision, dedication, and hard work.

Wayne Johnson, California political consultant extraordinaire, was instrumental in bringing together the coauthor team. For that a special thanks.

To Cindy Gibson, thank you for being there and keeping me focused, organized, and headed in the right direction.

Keith Korman and Heather Jackson displayed their indispensable skill at turning ideas into publishable text. My profound thanks.

On the personal side, thanks to my mother and father for their loving support, and to Alana and Alyssa for providing my inspiration. And a special thanks to Elizabeth Graham for sharing so much love, joy, and light in a challenging time.

—Joseph Farah
Sacramento, California

THIS LAND IS OUR LAND

Introduction

WHY YOU SHOULD CARE ABOUT
PROPERTY RIGHTS

*"The moment the idea is admitted into society that property is not as
sacred as the laws of God, and that there is not a force of law and public
justice to protect it, anarchy and tyranny commence."*

—JOHN ADAMS

Imagine you have just purchased a two-bedroom condo in New
York City. You had saved money for ten years to buy it. It is conveniently located, has a beautiful view, and you plan to turn one of
the bedrooms into a home office for your consulting business. You
paid $300,000 for the condo, but you are thrilled to have it.

After signing the check for the down payment, you are all set to
move in your furniture, computer, and personal effects. You hear a
knock at the door. Two armed agents from the U.S. Fish and Wildlife
Service (FWS) want to talk to you about your condo and your plans
to run a consulting business from that second bedroom. You see,
your condo has been designated as critical habitat for the endangered
Manhattan cockroach.

The Manhattan cockroach once roamed freely all over the island

1

of Manhattan, but human activities like the construction of high-rise condominiums, subways, and roads have reduced the habitat of the cockroach by over 98.5 percent. Their numbers have fallen drastically, according to a study done by a New York University graduate student in his apartment on Forty-third Street and Ninth Avenue. Last August, he discovered twenty roaches in a three-hour period. This year he could only locate ten. From this data, he requested that the roach be listed as an endangered species based on a 50 percent reduction in its population. Since no one submitted contrary claims to the FWS, it used this "best available data" and made the listing.

As a result, the FWS agents say that your second bedroom must be set aside for the cockroach. You are not allowed to put any furniture, clothes, or computer equipment in that room. You may not vacuum the floor in that room, as you may eliminate the roach's food supply. If you enter the room, you must be careful not to step on, harass, or intimidate any roaches that you might see. Turning on the light suddenly, for instance, frightens the roach and causes it to scurry away. If you do any of these things, it will be considered an unauthorized "taking" of the roach and you will be prosecuted to the full extent of the law—a year in prison and a $100,000 fine for each harassed roach.

In addition to setting aside your second bedroom for the roach, you must also allow for a "migration corridor" through your kitchen so that the roach may move from one habitat (your bedroom) to its next nearest habitat (the bedroom of the family next door). The agents inform you that the family next door used a vacuum cleaner in the roach's habitat, accidentally sucking up five roaches into the vacuum cleaner bag. The FWS brought charges, and when the family fought prosecution in court, the government subpoenaed their tax returns, immigration records, and old car rental receipts to see if they were good citizens. The family soon complied with all the provisions of the Endangered Species Act (ESA).

Being a good citizen yourself, you agree to the conditions, believing that you can live in harmony with one of God's creatures. Weeks pass, and you notice that the roaches are not content to remain in their habitat or in their migration corridor, but tend to get up into your grocery shelves. Your children are afraid to move around in the condo and the smell from the second bedroom is getting pretty bad. Since you cannot operate your consulting business from home, you rent office space. But the prices are so high, you soon have to give it up.

You decide that your condo is not worth the trouble, and decide to unload it. You go to a real estate agent to put it up for sale, but discover that since your condo was declared a critical habitat for the Manhattan cockroach, no one wants to live there. The best available offer is $25,000 from the Save the Cockroach Association of Manhattan (SCAM). SCAM is a nonprofit organization that buys up cockroach habitat. It bought your next door neighbor's condo for $25,000 and sold it to the federal government the next day for the original pre-habitat price of $300,000.

You find this a bit on the unethical side, but just before you take the $275,000 loss, your upstairs neighbor's waterbed bursts and floods your condo, completely annihilating the population of roaches. Believing it to be a sign from heaven, you begin to mop up in order to begin your life anew when you hear a knock at the door. There you find two armed agents of the U.S. Army Corps of Engineers. It appears your condo has just been designated a wetland.

Sound far-fetched? While admittedly a composite of government abuses and environmental horror stories, events very similar to those above have actually occurred to residents of western states. And while no cockroaches were involved, property owners and their families have had their lives and livelihoods ruined by endangered flies, beetles, rats, and shellfish.

"If urban residents were required to house the homeless the way rural residents have been required to house endangered species," wrote Ike Sugg of the Competitive Enterprise Institute (CIE), "per-

haps they would better understand the moral and economic outrage
that has catalyzed the property rights movement."

Suppose the local city council in your suburban neighborhood
decided that your backyard would be the perfect place for a "tot lot"
for all of the neighbors to use and ordered you to take down your
fence. Then the city came in and installed playground equipment in
your backyard. You would not stand for such an intrusion on your
rights. Well, westerners see even less justification for the government to seize their property to care for bugs.

URBAN JUNGLE

Perhaps you live in a large city and think you are beyond the reach
of wildlife regulation. Then you should know about one of the fastest
growing trends in wilderness conservation—"urban preserves."
There is a preserve run by the Nature Conservancy that lies entirely
within the city limits of Tulsa, Oklahoma. Space is set aside for
terns, which are sea birds, along the Arkansas River. "People know,"
said Neely Lowrie of the Tulsa Audubon Society. "They're aware of
the terns, look for them and respect the fact that for part of the year,
this river belongs to them."[1]

There are 150,000 acres of prairie, woodlands, and wetlands
within thirty minutes of Chicago's Loop. The area is home to 181
species listed as endangered or threatened in the state of Illinois. The
city has "forest preserve districts" in which volunteers are "helping
to set nature back on course" by restoring wilderness. Apparently,
wilderness needs a lot of upkeep—including pulling weeds. School
children are taken out to these urban preserves, blindfolded, and in-
structed to "hug a tree, feel its bark and figure out where the sun is."

---

1. All quotes and information about urban preserves from "Urban preserves meet the needs
of people and nature," *The Nature Conservancy,* September–October 1995.

In this way, the children are trained to establish an emotional attachment to the tree. Harvard University biologist Edward O. Wilson calls this feeling "biophilia." Children educated in this way are unlikely to think of trees in the same way they think of corn or cotton—as a renewable resource.

The Irvine Company Open Space Reserve is 17,000 acres of coastal sage scrub wilderness in the heart of Orange County, California and home to nearly a hundred threatened or endangered species. "The land was studied to determine what its needs were," said Steve Johnson, science director for the site, "before human considerations were taken into account." "Many people don't need or want to experience nature firsthand," volunteer Trish Smith explains, "but they like to see it and know it's there. They live in it vicariously."

By today's definitions, wilderness is not just a deeply forested area somewhere in the Rockies. The San Francisco Bay Wildlife Refuge—surrounding one of the largest cities in California—is the largest urban wildlife refuge in the United States, containing 21,000 acres of marshlands, salt ponds, and mudflats and four federally endangered species. Nearly 700 nests of egrets live on Shooters Island, a forty-five-acre nature preserve north of Staten Island in New York City—one of the most densely populated cities on the planet. About 13 percent of the island of Manhattan is designated as parkland or otherwise "protected." The wilderness is just outside your front door.

But even if you live in a completely urban environment and the only wildlife you encounter is at the local nightclub, *your* property rights—guaranteed to you by the Fifth Amendment to the U.S. Constitution—are under assault by government regulators and environmental zealots who believe that mankind brings only harm to his environment. If you own land, a business, a house, or have a financial interest in any of them, then you own *property*. And, as the Founding Fathers recognized when they drafted the Constitution, property rights are the foundation for all other civil rights guaranteed to us by that document. Without the freedom to acquire, possess, and defend property, all other guaranteed rights are merely words on a page.

Freedom of religion can be threatened if the government owns the church building. Freedom of the press can be threatened if the government owns the land upon which the printing press stands. Even freedom of speech is threatened if the government can foreclose on your house. It has been the practice of tyrants throughout history to seize the property and goods of an enemy. By taking away a person's property, you take away his rights and his ability to oppose you. Today, the government rarely sends soldiers armed with rifles to seize private property; it sends bureaucrats armed with regulations and environmental impact statements. But the result is the same.

The Endangered Species Task Force heard from the people whose lives are directly impacted by federal laws on wildlife and environmental protection. We traveled from coast to coast in March and April of 1995, holding a total of seven hearings. Over one hundred people testified—three-fourths of them had never testified before Congress. Hundreds more submitted written testimony. Over eight thousand people attended these hearings. We opened up the legislative process to more citizens in two months than in the previous twenty-two years, since the Endangered Species Act became law in 1973. We took Congress to the people, and it made the bureaucrats and lobbyists very nervous. The louder their complaints blared, the more we felt we were doing our job effectively.

Many politicians and commentators act as though the idea of property rights is a recent phenomenon. If it had not been for nationwide headlines about the Northern spotted owl, many urban residents might not be aware that there are people severely affected by environmental regulations and restrictions. In reality, the concept of property rights is as old as civilization itself.

The author of our Constitution, James Madison, wrote in 1792 that "as a man is said to have a right to his property, he may be equally said to have a property in his rights." What did he mean? Madison understood that there is a close correlation between property and rights. It may be as difficult to determine which came first, as it is with respect to the chicken and the egg. The founders understood that vital rights, such as freedom of speech and freedom of the press, actually descend from the understanding that people have an inherent and inalienable right to pursue and own property. For what are a person's ideas if not property?

Madison may have articulated this concept better than anyone in history, but he didn't invent the idea of property rights. In fact, he merely articulated the common knowledge of his time—a wisdom rooted in Roman law, in the Magna Carta, and in English common law. However, over the last century—and especially in the last two decades—property rights have been increasingly compromised and obscured by a growing body of federal, state, and local regulations and by open-ended Supreme Court decisions without standards or constitutional foundation.

It's time for a renaissance of thought, debate, and public policy action on property rights. That's what this book is intended to generate. In a society increasingly obsessed with rights, real and imagined, this most fundamental principle upon which our republic was built deserves to be fully restored as guaranteed by our Constitution. Let *This Land Is Our Land* serve as the manifesto—a declaration of not only what's wrong with current government policy toward private property, but how we can make it right. The stakes are high. And time is of the essence. Here's the opening salvo, then, in a revolution championing ownership over servitude and freedom over slavery.

1

THE HISTORY OF PROPERTY RIGHTS

*"Thus Joseph acquired all the farm land of Egypt for Pharaoh . . . and the
people were reduced to slavery, from one end of Egypt's territory
to the other."*

—GENESIS 47:20–21

Maybe the best way to begin is by defining "private property," and
by explaining its importance in any civil society. Private property
serves the same purpose for individuals as a national border serves
for a country. It delineates my land from your land. It defines the
geographic area of authority, responsibility, and power for the
owner. A property line distinguishes the area under my neighbor's
authority from that under my jurisdiction. That property line keeps
me free from my neighbor's whims, good intentions or bad, just as
the border, and the willingness to defend it, keep nations free from
the dictates of their neighbors.

Private property is also the legitimate boundary we draw to the
scope of governmental authority. In theory, my property is invio-
late as long as my actions do not violate the *rights* of others. Notice

8

we did not say "violate the *sensibilities* of others," or "violate the *enjoyment* of others," or even "violate the *interests of American society.*" This is a crucial point. Governments are justified in taking away or severely restricting property rights *only* if the exercise of those rights violates the rights of someone else. It is also important to remember that property rights, like all civil rights, are designed to protect the weak from the strong. Even the wealthiest and most powerful landowner is nothing compared to the full force of a national government. Property rights keep us free and independent, which is why so many of us seek to acquire property.

Property rights encompass *all* property, though common law distinguishes between real property (land, factories, etc.) and personal property (all other kinds, including intellectual property). Traditionally, property rights have been broken down into component parts. The most important of these are: 1) the right to possess; 2) the right to use; 3) the right to income; 4) the right to security; 5) the right to bequeath; 6) the right to deny harmful use; and 7) the right of liability.

WHAT ARE PROPERTY RIGHTS?

With the downfall of communism, it is difficult to find many people today who deny the existence of a right to *possess* property. Even the Russian constitution, drafted after the fall of the Soviet Union, states that "every person enjoys property rights, including the right to own, use and dispose of property, both individually and jointly with other individuals. Ownership rights are guaranteed by law. The inalienable right to own property guarantees personal individual interests and freedoms." Property possession is a right laid out in our oldest customs and traditions. But the other six property rights are just as important and need just as much protection. No one else has a *right* to your land or possessions. Your rights give you exclusive *use* of your property. No one else may legitimately use it without your permission. Your rights allow you to generate *income* from your property. Your rights allow you to *secure* your property—to defend it with fences, alarms, etc. Your rights allow you to *bequeath* your property to your heirs, indeed to pass your property rights on to your children and your descendants in perpetuity. Your rights allow you to *deny harmful use* of your property by others. In fact, your rights allow you to exclude others from your property even if their intentions are good. And lastly, your rights include *liability*. What occurs on your property is—for better or worse—ultimately your responsibility. That is how it should be.

The right to possess property is only one small part of property rights. If others dictate how you must use your property, or whether you can use it at all, then they have taken it from you. If others determine when and where you must provide access to your property, then they have taken it from you. If the actions of others prevent you from realizing income from your property, then they have taken it from you. If the actions of others prevent you from leaving your property to your children and your children's children, then they have taken it from you. And if others compel you to watch natural disasters destroy your property, then they have taken it from you. Whether those "others" are neighbors or local, state, or federal governments is irrelevant. Your civil rights, including those of property, are inalienable.

Property rights protect only property that is legitimately held. If a mugger steals your wallet, he does not then benefit from the protection of property rights. He has acquired his property illegitimately. The property does not belong to him. So, how do we determine what property belongs to whom? Roger Pilon of the Cato Institute provides an excellent answer: "To be legitimately held or owned, property must have been acquired without violating the rights of others. . . . something might have been acquired from the state of nature, in which it was unheld; more likely, it might have been acquired from someone else who held it legitimately, either in exchange for something else or as a gift; or it might have been ac- quired from someone else or his agent in rectification for some past wrong by that other. Thus, in general, do holdings and rights to the exclusive possession and use of those holdings arise legitimately. By contrast, things are held illegitimately when they are taken by force or fraud from those who hold them legitimately—that is, when they are taken without the voluntary consent of those who rightly hold them. When what is ours has been taken without our consent, our basic right to be free from interference in our persons and property has been violated. At bottom, then, rights violations are *takings.*"[1]

Takings is an issue for the next chapter, but Pilon goes on to ex- plain how and why conflicts arise over private property rights, and why they are such a concern today: "The property rights of some stand in the way of others' doing what they wish with that prop- erty—whether renting it at will, or at a controlled price, or deter- mining the numbers or kinds of structures that can be built upon it, or enjoying the view it affords, or whatever."

The usual response to this argument is that individual rights must defer to those of society as a whole. The rights of one person cannot overrule the "greater common good." But who judges what that greater good is and when it is to be applied? "Individually held property is used at the will of the owner, by right of the owner," writes Pilon. "The analogy to collectively held property breaks down, however, as soon as we realize that our collective rights over the property are informed by a collective will that simply does not exist . . . when we turn to the democratic device to try to settle how 'we' should use 'our' property, we face the notorious fact that that device rarely yields a majority preference."

Property rights go to the very heart of individual freedom. When

---

1. Roger Pilon, "Property Rights, Takings, and a Free Society," *Harvard Journal of Law and Public Policy,* Summer 1983.

others determine what will be done with your land and your goods, then you, the individual, became not only superfluous to the supposed "greater good" which will come from that determination, but you actually become an obstacle to that "greater good." It logically follows that obstacles to the "greater good" must be "evil," and therefore must be destroyed. This Manichaean thinking is inherent in tyrannical regimes ranging from ancient Peru to Maoist China. It doesn't matter whether that regime's intentions are to obtain personal wealth and power or to establish an idyllic natural paradise. The coercion is equally despotic.

PREHISTORIC ORIGINS

The concept of property rights has existed for as long as there has been property. In prehistoric times, people defended their property the same way animals do—by force. "Defending one's territory" is a concept easily seen by anyone who tries to remove a supper dish before his dog is finished eating. Animals also instinctively know that it is often much easier to take that which belongs to someone else than to produce or to capture it oneself. Humanity developed society, civilization, and laws to establish peaceful measures to resolve conflicts over property. These peaceful measures, along with a recognition of the rights of others, are what set us above the animal kingdom.

It is inherent in Judeo-Christian belief that God created the Earth and gave man dominion over it. God thus bestowed upon us our property rights and responsibilities. The right to property ownership transcends the authority of both government and man. But even if you do not subscribe to Judaic or Christian beliefs, the Bible, as a historical document, contains enough information to satisfy the most hardened atheist or agnostic of the existence of property rights from the beginning of recorded history.

The city of Jericho—even today the site of struggles between Jews and Arabs over deeds of ownership—has been a battleground over conflicting claims of property rights since biblical times. In *The Pelican History of the World,* J. M. Roberts writes: "For as long as we know there has been at Jericho a never-failing spring feeding what is still a sizable oasis. No doubt it explains why people have been there on and off for about ten thousand years. Farmers clustered about it in late prehistoric times; its population may then have numbered two or three thousand. Before 6,000 B.C. it had great water tanks which suggest provision for big needs, possibly for irrigation, and there was a massive stone tower which was part of elaborate defenses long kept in repair. Clearly its inhabitants thought they had something worth defending; they had property."[2]

The Book of Exodus is replete with God's laws concerning property damage and restitution: "When a man steals an ox or a sheep and slaughters or sells it, he shall restore four oxen for the one ox, and four sheep for the one sheep."[3] The idea that culminated in the "takings" provision of the Fifth Amendment appears in Exodus 22:4, along with an admonition about property responsibilities: "When a man is burning over a field or a vineyard, if he lets the fire spread so that it burns in another's field, he must make restitution with the best produce of his own field or vineyard."

The Book of Leviticus discusses the redemption and restoration of property, making it clear that human dignity is closely tied with the possession of one's own property. "When one of your fellow countrymen is reduced to poverty and is unable to hold out beside you, extend to him the privileges of an alien or a tenant, so that he may continue to live with you."[4]

The Catechism of the Catholic Church discusses the Seventh

---

2. J. M. Roberts, *The Pelican History of the World,* p. 57.
3. Exodus 21:37.
4. Leviticus 25:35.

Commandment ("Thou shall not steal") and draws the appropriate inferences from God's command. The Church tells us that the commandment requires "respect for the right to private property."[5] It also says that, "In the beginning God entrusted the earth and its resources to the common stewardship of mankind to take care of them, master them by labor, and enjoy their fruits."

The Church acknowledges the responsibilities which coincide with property rights: "The ownership of any property makes its holder a steward of Providence, with the task of making it fruitful and communicating its benefits to others, first of all his family." But it also states that governments cannot exempt themselves from deferring to property rights: "Even if it does not contradict the provisions of civil law, any form of unjustly taking and keeping the property of others is against the Seventh Commandment."

SECULAR UNDERPINNINGS

Along with moral and religious justifications for property rights, there are a great number of secular ones. The word "property" is derived from the Latin *proprius,* meaning "one's own." We need only look at the histories of ancient Greece and Rome to see efforts to avoid the centralized control of land. Both the Greeks and Romans experimented with various land reform efforts because they believed, correctly, that workers would be more productive if they worked their own land rather than that of the state or of large landowners. But forced redistribution of land by government did not solve the problem of inequity, it merely created an ongoing "necessity" to redistribute land. Circumstances change, and it was in-

---

5. This and following quotes from the Catechism of the Catholic Church, statements 2401ff.

evitable that some landowners would become more successful than others, buy more land, and become more powerful. As they did, they became the newest targets of redistribution. Landowners found this system arbitrary and often banded together. Many times they successfully defied the power of the state simply because of the independence that property gave them.

In ancient Athens, members of the council of the Areopagus found themselves able to overcome kingly power. Their land not only provided them with wealth, but with the surpluses necessary to provide arms, horses, and soldiers for the state. This gave them enough political power to defy, and sometimes usurp, the authority of Athenian kings. Homer describes these landowning elites as exhibiting a great deal of independence.

Plato's *Republic* describes the ideal, perfected human society. It is most noteworthy for the dictatorial restrictions that would have to be imposed upon human society in order to perfect it. The *Republic* is unstintingly authoritarian in nature, much like militaristic ancient Sparta, and removes most individual freedoms. But what is most interesting is to see how property rights fall on Plato's list of rights to be regulated or restricted. Plato's *Republic* would regulate marriages to produce the best genetic results. Families would be abolished. Culture and the arts would be censored. And private property would not exist. Thus Plato proved, in the negating of them, that private property rights are as important a freedom as those of association, privacy, and expression.

Other civilizations, remarkably different, illustrate the relationship between liberty and property. In ancient China, despite the belief that "under heaven every spot is the sovereign's ground," private property was a widespread practice. The Andean empire in South America was a formidably totalitarian society. The *Sapa Inca*— the "only Inca"—was a total despot. The population was organized into units from which labor and produce were exacted. Movement of the populace was strictly regulated, marriage outside the local community was forbidden, and, oh yes, all land and produce was state property.

As ancient civilizations gave way to feudalism and the Middle Ages, property and property rights became even more important. As described in *The Pelican History of the World*: "In this [feudal] world, possession of land or access to it was the supreme determinant of the social order. Somehow, slowly, but logically, the great men of western society, while continuing to be the warriors they had always been in barbarian societies, became landowners, too. With the dignitaries of the Church and their kings, they were the ruling class. From the possession of land came not only revenue by rent and taxation, but jurisdiction and labour service, too. Landowners were the lords, and gradually their hereditary status was to loom larger and their practical prowess and skill as warriors was to be less emphasized (though in theory it long persisted) as the thing that made them noble."[6]

COMMON LAW AND THE MAGNA CARTA

William the Conqueror cemented his rule of England in 1066 by retaining much land for himself and "leasing" the rest to his Norman associates. Ultimately, however, it was the ownership of land that enabled British nobility to place checks on the king's absolute power. On 15 June 1215, English barons forced King John to set his seal to the Magna Carta. Kings had previously recognized the rights of property, but the Magna Carta decreed that these rights existed despite the will of the king. The Great Charter established the principle that the king himself must govern according to law. It states:

---

6. Roberts, p. 399.

"No freeman shall be taken or imprisoned, or be disseised of his freehold, or liberties, or free customs, or be outlawed, or exiled, or any other wise destroyed; nor will we not pass upon him, . . . but by lawful judgement of his peers, or by the law of the land. We will sell to no man, we will not deny or defer to any man either justice or right."

Gottfried Dietz in *Magna Carta and Property* concluded that "the Great Charter was thus in a large measure prompted by the desire to have property rights protected. . . . By commemorating Magna Carta as a document of free government, we commemorate it as a charter of property."

In medieval Europe, landownership became the most important determinant of political power. This did not change even with the growth of a new merchant class. Successful merchants often bought land with the profits, so that their money could translate into social and political clout. By the time we reach the eighteenth century, we discover that "the landed class," particularly in England, has a great deal of influence on government policies. It was from these roots that America's Founding Fathers sprang.

Coupled with the growth of property as a political asset was the incessant growth of the state. From Rome to Byzantium to Paris to London—the machinery of government spread and grew. And as it grew, it required new sources of revenue to sustain itself. While taxes have been with us virtually as long as property has, government began looking more and more to land as the source of the wealth necessary to fulfill its needs. It was difficult to effectively tax commercial transactions or incomes, but land is immovable. Property is always within reach of the grasp of government. One of the most effective punishments against recalcitrant citizens throughout history has been the appropriation of lands by the state. One could still resist the government without property, but such resistance would be ineffective. Property was both the sword and shield of an independent class.

The French Revolutionaries spent a lot of time thinking and writing about rights—in between sending people to the guillotine. They saw no contradiction in promoting "the sanctity of property" while redistributing the lands of the church and aristocracy through the force of the state. This was pure democracy in action—the majority took what it wanted. Though the rich were the targets of this "appropriation," the architects of the policy soon became its victim. Equity, particularly of the material variety, could not be achieved through force. While the French Revolution ended unhappily, its abolition of serfdom had far-reaching effects. There were few serfs left in France in 1789, but the demise of the feudal system opened up the exploitation of land by the French peasantry. The correlation between the nationwide redistribution of property from the aristocracy to the peasantry and the nationwide "redistribution" of political power in the same direction is too obvious to overlook.

"LOST" RIGHTS

Eighteenth-century Britons were more philosophical about the importance of private property, but tended to be less diligent in practicing what they preached—especially in their American colonies. Author James Bovard, in his book *Lost Rights,* tells the story of the white pine laws in the early 1700s. The British used American pines as masts for their ships. This prompted Parliament to claim all the white pines in the colonies for the crown, forbidding settlers from cutting any down. Colonists in Maine were forced from their homes and their possessions burned for violating the timber laws. The king's agents also would seize white pines on the colonist's private property without offering compensation. Though mostly forgotten today, historians of the nineteenth century often cited the pine laws as the beginning of American disenchantment with British rule.

The great seventeenth-century philosopher John Locke summed up the essence of property rights in the phrase: "Lives, Liberties, and Estates, which I call by the general name, *Property.*"[7] Locke's ideas inspired many great thinkers to believe that property rights were so intertwined with life and liberty that they were worth defending— even to the point of outright rebellion against king and country. James Otis, a Boston lawyer, wrote in 1761: "A man's home is his castle; and whilst he is quiet he is as well guarded as a prince in his castle." Arthur Lee of Virginia commented in 1775: "The right of property is the guardian of every other right, and to deprive the people of this, is in fact to deprive them of their liberty." Some of these great thinkers in the colonies got together and wrote down their grievances. They felt they were on particularly solid ground when they accused King George III of these transgressions: "He has erected a Multitude of new Offices, and sent hither Swarms of Officers to harass our People, and eat out their Substance." Because of these grievous violations of their rights—specifically property rights— these colonists ratified a Declaration of Independence, a document which was, for all intents and purposes, a declaration of war against their duly constituted government.

There can be no doubt about how the Founders felt about property rights. They were unequivocal about it. John Adams, in his "Defense of the Constitutions of Government," wrote that "[P]roperty is surely a right of mankind as really as liberty. . . . The moment the idea is admitted into society that property is not as sacred as the laws of God, and that there is not a force of law and public justice to protect it, anarchy and tyranny commence."

For thousands of years, property rights had been evolving. Now they were to be enshrined in the founding documents of a new government—a republic whose three separate branches would prevent

---

7. John Locke, *The Second Treatise of Government,* § 123. 1965 edition.

one from establishing a tyranny. It would be a republic that would guarantee certain rights to the people: freedom of speech, freedom of religion, freedom of the press, freedom of association, the freedom to keep and bear arms. Finally, this republic would forbid unreasonable searches and seizures, and the taking of private property without just compensation. They enshrined these rights in the Constitution of the United States of America. Today, many American landowners want to know why they have to lobby Congress, write letters to federal agencies, and hold protests just to convince government officials that the Founders actually meant what they wrote in that document.

Satirist P. J. O'Rourke once remarked that the Founding Fathers would never make it in today's society because, two hundred years later, we can still understand what they meant. He may have been overly optimistic. The same people who have no difficulty finding all sorts of rights and privileges in the Constitution that are not written there, are unable to accept the existence of the ones that clearly are. These supporters of the "common good" have, all too often, turned the Constitution's commerce clause and the Ninth Amendment—provisions to enhance liberty—into tools to bludgeon Americans into submission.

2

THE CONSTITUTION: GRANITE OR PUTTY?

"Government is instituted no less for protection of the property, than of the persons of individuals. . . . The rights of property are committed into the same hands with the personal rights."

—James Madison, THE FEDERALIST NO. 54

The Constitution of the United States of America specifies exactly what the government's responsibilities are in relation to private property. An examination of the Founders' concerns and intentions is necessary to fully appreciate the warped interpretations made today by all three branches of government.

In May of 1776, the state of Virginia held a convention in support of independence. They asked one of their most prominent statesmen, George Mason, to draw up a Declaration of Rights and a new constitution. Mason's product, the Virginia Declaration of Rights, was the basis of the Declaration of Independence and the Constitution's Bill of Rights. The first section of the Declaration of Rights stated: "That all men are by nature equally free and independent and have certain inherent rights, of which, when they enter into a state of society, they cannot, by any compact, deprive or divest their posterity; namely the enjoyment of life and liberty, with the means of acquiring and possessing property, and pursuing and obtaining happiness and safety."

Mason's formulation was so upright and correct that twelve years later, during its state convention, Virginia proposed a Bill of Rights for the Constitution that included a near-verbatim use of Mason's words: "That there are certain natural rights, of which men, when they form a social compact, cannot deprive or divest their posterity: among which are the enjoyment of life and liberty, with the means of acquiring, possessing, and protecting property, and pursuing and obtaining happiness and safety." While the Framers of the Constitution decided not to reiterate the Declaration of Independence's trumpeting of inalienable or natural rights, they did incorporate property rights into the Fifth Amendment.

The U.S. Constitution is a remarkable document. Including the Bill of Rights, it is only 4,842 words long, but we manage to use it to run a nation of 260 million people more than 200 years after it was written. Of course, it takes a great deal of interpretation to cover situations the Framers never dreamed of in the late eighteenth century. Fortunately, our Founders were prolific writers and their words help us understand what they meant when they put together the Constitution.

If the letter and the spirit of the Constitution were being adhered to in America today, there would be no need for a "property rights movement," no talk of a "war on the West" and precious little dissatisfaction with the federal government. Through hundreds of hours of congressional testimony, and even more time listening to thousands of citizens complain about abuses by government, we have not heard a single suggestion that the problems lie with the Constitution.

A general discussion of constitutional revisionism is well beyond the scope of this book, but if we scrutinize the words of the Constitution and how they have bent to serve the opponents of property rights we can get a pretty good sense of where we need to head.

The preamble explains that the Constitution is established to, among other things, "promote the general welfare." Article 1, Section 8 gives Congress the power to "provide for . . . the general welfare." What do these broad statements mean? The phrase is taken from the Constitution's predecessor, the Articles of Confederation. The third article states that, "The said states hereby severally enter into a firm league of friendship with each other, for their common defence, the security of their liberties, and their mutual and general welfare . . ." In *The Federalist* No. 41, James Madison listed the "powers conferred on the Government of the Union" as security against foreign danger, regulation of the intercourse with foreign nations, maintenance of harmony and proper intercourse among the States, certain miscellaneous objects of general utility, restraint of the States from certain injurious acts, and provisions for giving due efficacy to all these powers.

The emphasis of the Founders was on the word "general" and not the word "welfare." The concern in 1788 was that weak and fragmented states might begin to squabble among themselves. Opponents of the new Constitution were fearful that a national government might see fit to choose sides in such disputes and use its constituted powers to promote the welfare of *specific* states. We tend to forget today that in the eighteenth century the governments of Pennsylvania, New York, Massachusetts, and Virginia were very different from each other. They were separated by long distances and the slow pace of eighteenth-century communications. The Constitution made it forcefully clear that the national government was to promote the *general* welfare—that states were not to be played off one against the other. This is supported by later provisions that say: "No preference shall be given by any regulation of commerce or revenue to the ports of one state over those of another. . . ."

How could such a simple concept become a threat to property rights? The interpretations of legislators, executives, interest groups, and judges over the past two centuries have used the term "general welfare" to circumvent the one consistent problem activists and social engineers find with the Constitution. It is a Constitution of *enumerated* powers (more on this when we reach the Tenth Amendment). When there is no authorization in the Constitution for government to perform a certain function, its last refuge is to claim it is "promoting the general welfare." This leads to legal disputes that work their way through the court system until they find judges like the one in *Lionshead Lake v. Township of Wayne,* who concluded:

"Has a municipality the right to impose minimum floor-area requirements in the exercise of its zoning power? Much of the proof adduced by the defendant Township was devoted to showing that the mental and emotional health of its inhabitants depended upon the proper size of their homes. We may take notice without formal proof that there are minimums in housing below which one may not go without risk of impairing the health of those who dwell therein. . . . But quite apart from these considerations of public health which cannot be overlooked, minimum floor-area standards are justified on the grounds that they promote the general welfare of the community. . . ."[1]

Such judicial meanderings do not start and end in New Jersey. Supreme Court Justice William O. Douglas wrote this opinion in 1954: "We do not sit to determine whether a particular housing project is or is not desirable. The concept of the public welfare is broad and inclusive. . . . It is within the power of the legislature to determine that the community should be beautiful as well as healthy, spacious as well as clean, well-balanced as well as carefully patrolled. . . . Once the question of the public purpose has been

1. *Lionshead Lake v. Township of Wayne,* 10 N.J. 165, 173, 89 A.2d 693, 697 (1952).

decided, the amount and character of the land to be taken for the project and the need for a particular tract to complete the integrated plan rests in the discretion of the legislative branch."[2]

Thus we find a justice of the United States Supreme Court promoting the idea that the public welfare gives the legislature the power to mandate a "well-balanced" community. A well-balanced community can be anything a bureaucrat wants it to be. Property rights necessarily suffer under such a formulation.

THE COMMERCE CLAUSE

Article 1, Section 8 of the Constitution says: "The Congress shall have power . . . to regulate commerce with foreign nations, and among the several states, and with the Indian tribes. . . ." Amazingly, this Commerce Clause has become the catchall justification for all sorts of federal intrusions—from environmental regulation to gun laws to school curricula. Only recently has the Supreme Court held that Congress has taken its Commerce Clause powers too far.

In *U.S. v. Lopez,* the Court ruled that the possession of a gun in a local school zone is in no sense an economic activity that might, through repetition elsewhere, have a substantial effect on interstate commerce. While *Lopez* was unrelated to property rights, the arguments of U.S. attorneys prosecuting the case illustrate a profound misunderstanding of the Constitution. Chief Justice William Rehnquist noted that under the government's reasoning, "Congress could regulate any activity that it found was related to the economic productivity of individual citizens . . . we are hard-pressed to posit any activity by an individual that Congress is without power to regulate." Justice Clarence Thomas reported: "When asked at oral argument

---

2. Justice Douglas in *Berman v. Parker,* 348 U.S. 26, 33, 35, 36 (1954).

if there were *any* limits to the Commerce Clause, the Government was at a loss for words. . . . Such a formulation of federal power is no test at all: it is a blank check."

The Commerce Clause means exactly what it says, that Congress can regulate interstate commerce. There is no mystery about it. This was intended to prevent contentious states from treating each other as if they were foreign countries. The Commerce Clause's effect on privately owned land and property should be minimal. It should never be used as a justification to declare someone's property "critical habitat" or "wetland" or "a landmark." The Supreme Court once ruled that the wheat a farmer grew for his own use could be regulated by Congress because it could *potentially* be sold across state lines and thus affect interstate commerce. The Constitution is *not* what the Supreme Court says it is, but what the Constitution itself says it is.

THE BILL OF RIGHTS

The Bill of Rights and subsequent constitutional amendments set out for all those rights that cannot be taken away by the dictates of the majority. The Third, Fourth, Fifth, Ninth, Tenth, and Fourteenth Amendments all have significant provisions concerning property rights.

The Third Amendment is not often cited by civil libertarians these days: "No Soldier shall, in time of peace be quartered in any house, without the consent of the Owner, nor in time of war, but in a manner to be prescribed by law." The quartering of troops in private homes is certainly not a widespread practice today, but Congress has no qualms about forcing private citizens to provide habitat for animals. While we are not suggesting that the Endangered Species Act be challenged on Third Amendment grounds, it is illustrative of the Founders' intentions regarding the sanctity of private property.

The Fourth Amendment protects us from the physical encroachments of government: "The right of the people to be secure in their persons, houses, papers, and effects, against unreasonable searches and seizures, shall not be violated, and no Warrants shall issue, but upon probable cause, supported by Oath or affirmation, and particularly describing the place to be searched, and the persons or things to be seized." In fact, property owners are not secure from unreasonable searches and seizures, as will be evident when we get to the discussion of Lemhi County, Idaho, and Eugene Hussey. This seventy-four-year-old rancher was threatened and intimidated by armed Fish and Wildlife agents while searching for the bullet that killed a wolf. The Fish and Wildlife Service is not authorized to obtain and execute a search warrant in such a case. Considering that the Founders were fearful of "standing armies," they would certainly have been startled by the fact that the Fish and Wildlife Service, the Environmental Protection Agency, and the National Marine Fisheries Service all have their own private, armed, enforcement agents.

The Fifth Amendment was the Founders' main defense of property rights: ". . . nor shall any person . . . be deprived of life, liberty, or property, without due process of law; nor shall private property be taken for public use, without just compensation." The Founders were not anarchists. They foresaw instances when government would need to take possession of private land "to provide for the general welfare"—for instance, when building the interstate highway system. So they included a provision for "just compensation" when private property is taken for public use. Forcing someone to give over his land for wildlife habitat is without question a taking for public use. It requires just compensation. In the *National Gazette* of 27 March 1792, James Madison wrote: "That is not a just government, nor is property secure under it, where the property which a man has in his personal safety and personal liberty, is violated by arbitrary seizures of one class of citizens for the service of the rest." Madison goes on to say that a government that *directly or indirectly* violates property rights "is not a pattern for the United States." This flies in the face of those who claim that the Fifth Amendment only covers outright condemnation of land, or exercise of eminent domain.

As an experiment, Representative Don Young (R-Alaska) wanted to discover if the U.S. government of today violated Madison's tenets for the protection of private property. He asked the Congressional Research Service to provide a list of federal laws and regulations that more or less *directly* affect the use of privately owned land. Congressman Young was startled by the sheer number of federal justifications available for violation of the Fifth Amendment:

- The Comprehensive Environmental Response, Compensation and Liability Act (CERCLA)
- The Endangered Species Act
- The Surface Mining Control and Reclamation Act
- The Wilderness Act of 1964
- The Mining in the National Parks Act
- The Clean Water Act
- The Coastal Zone Management Act
- The Clean Air Act
- The National Historic Preservation Act
- The Coastal Barrier Resources Act
- The Safe Drinking Water Act
- Cape Cod National Seashore Act
- Wild and Scenic Rivers Act
- National Trails System Act
- Columbia River Gorge National Scenic Area Act

The number of federal laws that can *indirectly* affect private land could number in the thousands—the Desert Protection Act springs immediately to mind.

As for the government's power of eminent domain, Roger Pilon of the Cato Institute points out that this is not carte blanche for governments to do as they please: "There is no *private* right of eminent domain, nor could there be a *public* right either, for, again, individuals cannot give to the state rights they do not first have to give. What justification the power of eminent domain enjoys, then, must be taken from considerations of necessity, which are compelling only in exceptional cases and never from considerations of right. In those cases, moral theory requires, as a matter of simple justice, that whatever inroads the state must make on private rights must be accompanied by just compensation, compensation that in truth should reflect not only the physical but the moral facts of the matter as well. Given these moral facts about the power of eminent domain, then, there exists a strong presumption *against* its use and, once the burden has shifted to the state, a heavy burden of proof before it is used."[3]

Many restrictions placed on property by the government are illegitimate and should not be allowed, whether compensated or not. Failing that, those restricted should at least be compensated. Public goods should be paid for by the public. As Pilon explains, except when issues of endangerment arise, regulations of lot sizes, set-back requirements, or restrictions on types of construction are all illegitimate. These uses take nothing that belongs to others and hence violate no rights. He continues:

"We have no rights to preserve particular neighborhood styles, for example, not unless we create those rights through private covenants. Likewise with rent controls or

---

3. Pilon.

antidiscrimination measures: private individuals have a perfect right to offer their properties for sale or rent to whomever they choose at whatever prices they wish. For neither discrimination, on whatever grounds, nor offers, of whatever kind, can be shown to take what belongs free and clear to others; opportunities that depend upon the holdings of others, though perhaps measurable as a matter of *costs,* are not themselves freely held and hence are not objects of *rights.* Again, not even regulations that preserve private views can be justified if those regulations prohibit activities otherwise legitimate. For a view does not 'belong' to someone unless he owns all the conditions of the view; views that run over the property of others, even lovely ones, are not 'owned' but are merely 'enjoyed' at the pleasure of those others, who have a perfect right to block them by exercising any of their own freely held uses. In general, whether it is a view, a certain neighborhood style, or whatever, these and other such goods have to be wholly owned in order to be secured as a matter of right. Asking the government to step in to fully secure these goods is nothing less than acquiring them by taking what rightly belongs to others. If the individual has no right to do this on his own, then he has no right to do it through the government."[4]

Of course, not everyone reads the Fifth Amendment the way you or I do. Representative Chet Edwards (D-Texas) once said in a floor debate that the takings clause "is not an absolute right like freedom of speech or freedom of the press. Of course it is not; otherwise you would bankrupt government." Environmental attorneys Christopher J. Duerksen and Richard J. Roddewig, while admitting that the right to private property is "one of the most fundamental of individual

---

4. Ibid.

rights," can still sermonize that "taxpayers need not subsidize unwise development." Duerksen and Roddewig make their living deciding on behalf of their clients if your development is "unwise."[5] Wise or unwise, when the government places restrictions on a landowner, it has the responsibility to ensure that such laws are equitable and the public benefits derived from the restrictions are paid for by the entire public, and not shouldered by a few whose only "crime" is that they own property.

The Ninth Amendment states: "The enumeration in the Constitution, of certain rights, shall not be construed to deny or disparage others retained by the people." The purpose of this amendment was to acknowledge that the Constitution is not an exhaustive list of what the people are allowed to do or say. State constitutions, for example, may provide citizens with other rights. But revisionist interpretations have allowed activists to claim that the Ninth Amendment turns just about anything into a constitutional right. The Constitution is silent on such things as air rights, water rights, downstream rights, view rights, historic landmarks, etc. Such rights may be considered constitutional if found in state or local law, but *only* if they do not interfere or encroach upon the rights enumerated in the U.S. Constitution. Again, the Ninth Amendment is a limitation on federal power, not carte blanche for states, municipalities, and private organizations to circumvent the Bill of Rights.

The Tenth Amendment, currently experiencing a renaissance of interest after being ignored for so many years, states: "The powers not delegated to the United States by the Constitution, nor prohibited by it to the States, are reserved to the States respectively, or to the people." What could be more clear and concise? The states and the people retain all power not bestowed upon the federal government. In *Federalist* 45, James Madison makes a blunter statement:

---

5. "An Introduction to Takings Law & the Historical Background of Takings," by Duerksen and Roddewig published on Natural Resources Defense Council web page.

"The powers delegated by the proposed Constitution to the federal government are few and defined. Those which are to remain in the State governments are numerous and indefinite."

The Tenth Amendment is the reason that the coalition of supporters of centralized government and environmental causes is forced to resort to such dodges as the Commerce Clause to justify their actions. If James Madison were alive today, and he stepped into the offices of the Fish and Wildlife Service to remind its officials that the federal government's powers are "few," he would be laughed out of the building. The Constitution recognizes the States as separate sovereign entities and limits the federal government to regulating relations between them—promoting the *general* welfare and regulating commerce *among the states*. To justify the current level of federal intrusion into private lives and property is to turn the Constitution on its head. As Clarence Thomas remarked in *U.S. v. Lopez,* "Our case law could be read to reserve to the United States all powers not expressly *prohibited* by the Constitution."

Finally, the Fourteenth Amendment, ratified in 1868, states: ". . . nor shall any State deprive any person of life, liberty, or property, without due process of law . . ." This amendment is a limitation on the power of States. The Bill of Rights was established to ensure that the national government would not violate the rights to life, liberty, and property. The Fourteenth Amendment declares that individual States cannot do so either. We are immediately reminded of the promises made to freed slaves during Reconstruction: "40 acres and a mule." That really resonated with a freed slave. Freedom of speech was wonderful, the right to keep and bear arms was necessary, and the right to trial by jury was crucial, but the one thing that freed slaves knew would firmly establish their new liberty was property. Notice that this protection still required a constitutional amendment because it was not enumerated in the original document. One must advance to the twentieth century before one sees the proposition that the Constitution is "a living document." This is a fancy expression which means the Constitution does not mean what it says. But it does. It was not written in pencil.

A full understanding of the Constitution cannot be complete without examining the arguments of the opponents of our founding documents, known as the anti-federalists. The Constitutional Convention was convened because the Articles of Confederation left the national government too weak to settle disputes among the states and left it at the mercy of the whims of powerful states. More centralized authority was needed. But men such as Patrick Henry and Melancton Smith were worried about what would happen once the central government got a taste of real power. In his introduction to the Anti-Federalist Papers, Ralph Ketcham of Syracuse University noted: "The anti-federalists were, in a sense, 'men of little faith' as both contemporary and modern critics have charged, but this was true only within their fear that centralized power tended to become arbitrary and impersonal."

Federal power, particularly as it relates to property, *has* become arbitrary and impersonal. It is the cause of much controversy and upheaval throughout the nation. The anti-federalists were right—but at the wrong time. If Patrick Henry were still around, he would be the Republican nominee for president. And if he were elected, his first act might be to overhaul completely the most arbitrary and impersonal powers now exercised by the federal government—those associated with the Endangered Species Act.

3

WHO'S REALLY ENDANGERED?

"I am so tired of this legislation by anecdote. Everywhere you turn there is some poor farmer who lost their acres because there were kangaroo rats on it."

—DENNIS MURPHY, DIRECTOR OF STANFORD UNIVERSITY'S CENTER FOR CONSERVATION BIOLOGY

The current Endangered Species Act is fast approaching its twenty-fifth birthday, and has been due for a rewrite since 1992. Like many other conservation laws, it has become outdated and outmoded by advances in science and technology. Numerous scientific experts have recognized that there are some species that should not be listed and other species that simply cannot be saved. At the same time, the act has been inflicting a disproportionate amount of sacrifice—human, economic, and social—at an enormous cost.

In 1973, President Richard Nixon signed the Endangered Species Act into law. The sponsors of the act had the noble intention of saving grizzly bears, bald eagles, and alligators. What they failed to take into account was that there were millions of species in the world, including 30 million species of insects, a million and a half of fungi, and tens of millions of bacteria.

Under the Endangered Species Act, federal protection is provided to species listed as endangered or threatened. Any species or subspecies of fish, wildlife, or plants may be listed, as well as geographically distinct populations of vertebrate species. This is an important distinction for the layman to understand. The ESA could be invoked to protect one subspecies, even though others may be plentiful, or even overpopulated.

The secretary is supposed to adopt regulations that rely on the "best scientific and commercial data available" after considering the status of the species and efforts being made to protect the species. But only decisions not to list are subject to judicial review. While the original act intended that there be a legal distinction between a threatened and endangered species, in reality, this distinction has been blurred through the regulatory process.

In theory, the ESA saves species from the depredations of humankind and restores them to viable populations. In actuality, it violates property rights and has arguably resulted in the recovery of *no* species. It has cost the United States billions of dollars—not only in direct costs, but in lost opportunity costs for economic growth. What is worse, the authorization for the act expired on 30 September 1992. Since that time, property rights have been abrogated under the authority of an expired law.

As of this writing, there are 964 endangered species listed in the United States with another 4,100 candidate species awaiting a listing decision. Any concerned citizen with a stamp and a postcard can petition the Department of Interior's Fish and Wildlife Service (FWS) to list any population of plant, animal, or microorganism under the ESA. Candidate species are usually designated by a Fish and Wildlife biologist, normally in a field office, without formal proceedings, scientific investigation, or peer review of biological data.

Once a species is listed, the FWS drafts a recovery plan for it. The FWS has estimated that *each* recovery plan will cost $2 million, and it takes at least ten years to delist a species.

The Endangered Species Act makes it a crime to "take" a species listed as endangered. It goes on to define "take" as "to harass, harm, pursue, hunt, shoot, wound, kill, trap, capture or collect." A recent Supreme Court decision in *Sweet Home v. Babbitt* broadly defines the term "harm" to include any modification to habitat that might "impair essential biological functions." Policing the ESA is a big job. The FWS is responsible for wildlife and its habitats in 491 refuges over approximately 91 million acres. There are very few limits to the power of the FWS to protect species. Arrayed against this juggernaut of federal force are farmers, ranchers, and homeowners. They are people with a plot of land trying to fulfill their version of the American dream.

Though the Endangered Species Act permeates every corner of every state in the Union, California has become the main battleground because of the nearly 1,200 listed and candidate species there. Here are just a few of the problems ESA has caused in recent years. These accounts highlight the flaws of the act as it currently stands.

THE COASTAL CALIFORNIA GNATCATCHER

In 1988, Jonathan Atwood published a study describing a new species of bird—the California gnatcatcher. The data upon which the study was based was part of Atwood's Ph.D. dissertation. Atwood divided the species into two subspecies—*Polioptila californica californica* in the north, and *Polioptila californica margaritae* in the south. He divided the two ranges at 25 degrees north latitude. The vast majority of the approximately 2.5 million gnatcatchers were in the northern "coastal" subspecies.

36

In 1990, however, Atwood published a new report that moved the southern limit of the coastal gnatcatcher subspecies' range to 30 degrees latitude. This maneuver made almost 2.5 million gnatcatchers magically disappear into the Mexican subspecies. Overnight, there were only about 2,000 pairs of coastal gnatcatchers left. Not so coincidentally, this number is considered a "minimum viable population" under the ESA, qualifying the coastal gnatcatcher for listing. In March 1993, the FWS listed the coastal California gnatcatcher as a threatened species. This "ornithological gerrymandering," as environmental analyst Ike Sugg called it, conveniently put huge amounts of Southern California coastline under the jurisdiction of the FWS.

The Building Industry Association of Southern California asked to see the data upon which Atwood's new findings were based. The FWS repeatedly refused to provide the data. So the association sued U.S. Secretary of the Interior Bruce Babbitt. Secretary Babbitt claimed that the FWS used Atwood's *study* to list the gnatcatcher, not the data, and therefore was not required to make the data available for public inspection. Judge Stanley Sporkin of the D.C. District Court disagreed and invalidated the gnatcatcher listing in 1994.

Judge Sporkin ordered Dr. Atwood to provide the data and he did—but, not the original raw data. The raw data were discarded in 1986 when Atwood moved from California to Massachusetts. Also discarded were the computer programs Atwood used to analyze the data for his articles. Atwood "cannot recall with 100 percent certainty whether my earlier analyses included rounding of any of the data values provided here." Due to these uncertainties (and the possibility of "subtle programming errors"), Atwood explains: "I consider it likely that any reanalysis of the data . . . will yield results that differ slightly from those published in my 1988 and 1991 papers."

Backing up to a second line of defense, Atwood pointed out that his study only examined geographic variation in male gnatcatchers, while (conveniently) a new study by Drs. Mellink and Rea concluded that the difference is greater in females.

One of the ways to differentiate between gnatcatcher types is to examine the color of their plumage. Atwood used a spectrophotometer, a device used to quantify coloration differences, on the gnatcatchers. Now, Mellink and Rea have concluded that "the spectrophotometer, designed to measure the colors of flat and uniform surfaces, seems ill-suited for the variable texture of feathers."

What we are left with, then, are two different subspecies of birds, whose range of habitat changed by 345 miles in three years, based on scientific data that is now lost, and spectrophotometer readings that are "ill-suited" for differentiating plumage colors. Upon this mighty cornerstone, the FWS tried to set aside thousands of acres of Southern California coastland—not to mention the thousands of dollars the U.S. government spent to defend its indefensible position.

THE DELHI SANDS FLOWER LOVING FLY

Greg Ballmer has a master's degree in entomology and has worked for twenty years as a staff research associate for the department of entomology at the University of California at Riverside. While his work deals mainly with helping farmers eradicate pests, his hobby is the investigation of rare insect species. In October 1989, Ballmer petitioned the FWS to list as an endangered species the *Rhaphiomidas terminatus abdominalis* or Delhi Sands Flower Loving Fly. Ballmer claimed that nearly all extant populations were located within a 5,000-acre patch that included portions of the cities of Colton, Rialto, and San Bernardino.

The Delhi Sands Flower Loving Fly, Ballmer informed the FWS, is about one inch long. It flies low to the ground (landing frequently) and hovers like a hummingbird over flowers. Its adult life span in nature is "about one week, although under ideal conditions in captivity they have been kept alive for up to two weeks." While Ballmer clearly knew more about the fly than any other person in the state, his ignorance about the fly's biological habits was breathtaking: "The biology of *R.t. abdominalis* is not well known . . . feeding has not been observed for *R.t. abdominalis* . . . Larval development is not reported . . . specific vegetational requirements are not known."

Despite this lack of hard data, Ballmer had no shortage of conclusions or recommendations: "Since no data are available to indicate actual historic population levels of this species, the best estimate of population trends must be based on the extent of occupied habitat. . . . Current populations of this species occupy about 2.5 percent of the total area of Delhi series soil in this region. On the basis of habitat loss, approximately 97.5 percent of all *R.t. abdominalis* have been eliminated." Ballmer suggested that FWS designate the area as critical habitat and that "good environmental planning often incorporates wildlife linkages (habitat corridors) to connect patches of habitat which separately may be too small to maintain populations of the organisms of concern." His solution for fly management? "[I]t is highly unlikely that landowners will voluntarily act to preserve habitat for this species. The most likely means of preserving sufficient habitat for this species seems to be the establishment of a Habitat Conservation Plan to identify critical habitat and funding sources to purchase it." And then the pièce de résistance: "A likely possibility for such funding is a tax on future development within the historic range of this species."

It is difficult to tell what the FWS did with Ballmer's original request, but in 1992, when he requested the fly be listed on an emergency basis, the service took action. The FWS set up public hearings and asked for written comments. In the meantime, industrial development around the town of Colton was put on hold. The counties of San Bernardino and Riverside had put together a joint public-private development project to promote growth and employment in the recession-sluggish area. Local governments provided tax and economic incentives to encourage businesses to invest there. Ballmer's fly put a stop to all that. It wasn't until much later that Dr. William Hazeltine, an environmental consultant with over thirty years of experience in entomology, took a look at Ballmer's petition. "The Petition for Emergency Listing of this subspecies as endangered by Ballmer seems a little 'gassy' and overdone," he said.

The FWS public hearing was held in January 1993 in San Bernardino. The majority of testimony opposed listing. The FWS received fifty-seven written comments concerning the fly. One note, signed "a concerned citizen," simply said "You guys are NUTS!" Over 81 percent of the comments received opposed listing, with 16 percent in support. This does not include a petition with forty-eight signatures opposing the listing, circulated by an ad hoc committee of San Bernardino citizens called "People for Responsible Environmentalism."

Ballmer's supporters were few and far between. Despite the presence of forty-nine Ph.D.s in the UC Riverside entomology department, no one from the university testified in support of the listing. On the contrary, the university made it clear that the fly was Ballmer's baby alone. The intellectual level of advocacy for the fly is best illustrated by the words of Albert Kelley of the Craft and Hills Open Space Conservancy, who testified: "The Delhi fly may hold the key to our survival."

After months of deliberation, the final ruling of the FWS was released on 22 September 1993. The Delhi Sands Flower Loving Fly was listed as an endangered species. Ballmer's information was utilized exclusively by the FWS to justify its decision. In the ruling, FWS said that it "strongly believes that economic considerations have no relevance to determinations regarding the status of species. . . ." The county's plans to develop sixty-nine acres of unoccupied habitat would have to be stalled because it "would sever an important link between adjacent patches of occupied habitat." The service acknowledged "that more precise scientific information will benefit the fly's recovery, but it is not a legitimate basis for postponing a listing decision." Not only that, but the FWS made it clear that even attempting to find out more about the fly could be harmful: "Even scientific collecting, or repeated handling and marking could eliminate or seriously damage the populations through loss of genetic variability."

The listing caused San Bernardino County to spend $3.3 million to redraw plans for a new hospital in Colton, because of the presence of *eight* flies. That money totals the average cost of treatment for 23,644 outpatients. What is more, it wasn't until after the listing decision had been made that Ballmer's petition and supporting documentation was made available to the public. Only then did listing opponents discover that the documentation was long on doomsday predictions and short on hard evidence.

Ballmer claimed that the fly's habitat was one-half the area present in 1975, but offered no citation to support his claim. Riverside County Farm Bureau environmental manager Dennis Hollingsworth complained to the FWS that "there is no indication that the Service, or the petitioner, or anyone else has even attempted a comprehensive survey of the two counties, the general area, or even the extent of the Delhi Sands soil type. . . . It is apparent from the lack of knowledge on the life cycle of this species, and the absence of even a single observation of reproduction, hatching, or feeding that habitat requirements for the fly are also not well known. . . . The statement that . . . 97 percent of the habitat of the fly has been eliminated is even less credible and entirely without basis. . . . The assertion that the fly is being overutilized by collectors is pure speculation not supported by fact."

Ballmer's petition stated that "the largest one-day number of *R.t. abdominalis* observed during 1989 was on approximately 20 acres near Slover Mountain where an intense survey by three searchers disclosed 13 individual [flies]." In fact, estimates of the fly's population were based on a five man-hour survey done in 1989 on twenty acres around Slover Mountain. In other words, Ballmer and two friends spent one hour and forty minutes in an area some 300 yards wide by 300 yards long—no doubt on their hands and knees searching for the low-flying insect—and observed thirteen flies during that time. Such methodology, determining the fly was endangered, could legitimately claim that mosquitoes are endangered species.

The law requires the FWS to use the "best available data" for its listing decisions. "This has the appropriate acronym B.A.D.," explained Robert Gordon, executive director of the National Wilderness Institute. "The FWS is under no obligation to independently verify the data or the qualifications of a listing requester."

Under fire by cartoonists and columnists for the fly decision, Mollie Beattie, director of Fish and Wildlife Service, defended the listing. "[N]early all of its historic habitat has been destroyed, and it currently inhabits a mere 350 to 700 acres in an area of sandy soils in Southern California known as the Delhi Formation," she said. She was, of course, defending the decision with a claim made exclusively by Ballmer, and not supported by any independent data.

Ballmer himself seemed to understand that the data was flimsy. In an update of the fly's status, he used qualifying words ("may," "possibly," "perhaps," "roughly," etc.) seventy-six times in a four-and-one-half-page letter to the San Bernardino County Administrative Office. In the midst of the flower-loving fly controversy, Ballmer put on his pith helmet and found three more "endangered species" in the same area as the fly—a butterfly, a cricket, and a cockroach. "If we're going to hold up a multi-million dollar project because of a cockroach, we have gone way past unreasonable," said county supervisor Jerry Eaves.

Who's Really Endangered?

THE TIPTON KANGAROO RAT

Taiwanese emigrant Taung Ming-Lin learned a lot about the state of individual liberty in the United States. The Kern County, California, farmer drew nationwide media attention when he allegedly ran over four or five endangered Tipton kangaroo rats while plowing his fields. In February 1994, some twenty armed federal and state Fish and Wildlife agents descended on Lin's farm and seized the "murder weapon"—his tractor. He was charged with three misdemeanor counts of violating the Endangered Species Act. He could have lost nearly half of his 723 acres and been fined $600,000.

Supporters of property rights took up Lin's cause and journalists had a field day writing about government agencies run amok. Government bureaucrats do not like to look foolish. So, rather than do the honorable thing and quietly drop their prosecution of Lin, the Feds rolled out their heavy artillery.

U.S. Attorney Charles J. Stevens filed a "notice of intention to offer impeachment evidence" against Lin with the U.S. District Court in Fresno. The government announced its intention that, should Lin testify in his own behalf, it would introduce evidence attacking his credibility. None of this evidence, of course, had any direct relationship to whether Lin knowingly and with malice aforethought ran over Tipton kangaroo rats with his tractor. The notice showed that the government prosecutors intended to make an example of Lin by raising questions about his immigration status, his tax returns—even his California driver's license.

Federal prosecutors claimed that Lin was convicted of a "fault injury" in Taiwan in 1987 and was sentenced to four months in prison. Specifics were not given, but the filing implied that the "crime" related to "felony convictions for crimes of violence." The government also claimed that Lin was being sought by Taiwanese authorities for a 1994 fraud offense.

As it turned out, none of this was true, but U.S. Attorney

Stevens continued. He planned to introduce "evidence of untruth-fulness." The U.S. District Court ordered the Internal Revenue Service to turn over Li's tax returns to the U.S. Attorney's Office. The prosecution thus learned that Lin filed no federal tax return for tax years 1990 through 1993. Lin's 1990 tax return "contained false statements," according to the filing. Lin's heinous lies? He had "misrepresented his name and marital status."

Lin reported a 1990 total income of $5,726. But the Feds claimed that Lin deposited $82,000 in a three-month period in 1990. How did they know? They obtained Lin's bank records (try to remember that Lin was charged with three misdemeanors for *running over rats while farming*). The government claimed that Lin lied under oath in a 1992 superior court debt case when he claimed he had three children, all female. The government said Lin had four children, including one son whom the government subpoenaed as a material witness.

Lin testified that he was unemployed. But the prosecutors say Lin later claimed he was employed during this period. How do they know? They found it in Lin's 1993 *car lease application*. The government claimed that Lin may have been an illegal alien. Prosecutors said that he applied for amnesty status in 1990. To be eligible, the applicant must have illegally entered the United States prior to 1 January 1982. The government said that Lin's previous statements indicated he only arrived in 1990. Government prosecutors claimed Lin made false statements in his application for an identification card from the California Department of Motor Vehicles and they also inquired into Mrs. Lin's bank accounts.

The government was not required to release this "evidence" in advance, so why did it do so? Prosecutors claimed it was "to allow the court the opportunity to deal with this important issue prior to the commencement of the trial." Anthony Capozzi, Lin's attorney, disagreed. "This is an attempt to intimidate my client," he said. "There is no doubt about it."

Property rights supporters went through the roof. They sent faxes and letters and organized protests. Lin, as a *Wall Street Journal* editorial put it, "was hardly some sort of hardened toxics-dumping, stream-polluting eco-criminal to be made an example of. . . ." Certainly this wasn't Charles Manson. Ultimately, Lin and the government settled the case. Newspaper editorials were harshly critical of the government. The Fish and Wildlife Service couldn't understand the uproar over what apparently is business as usual for them. Michael J. Spear, regional director of the FWS complained: "Here are the facts: We made at least five attempts to gain Lin's compliance with the law before serving a search warrant. We mounted no effort to discredit Lin in the news media. In the midst of intense media demands at the time, our statements were conservative, measured and respectful of Lin's rights as a defendant. The allegations referred to in the editorial were public court records, provided at reporters' request. We made no 'mean-spirited' attempt to intimidate Lin by having his driver's license suspended. As a routine part of the investigation, it came to light that he had filed for licenses under several names, and that discovery was brought to the attention of the DMV. We did not 'decide to go after [Lin's] wife and daughter.' The government filed against the corporation, and it's standard legal practice to name the officers of a corporation in such actions. The bottom line is that, as a part of the settlement agreement, Lin has agreed to obey the law, which is all we sought in the first place. The Fish and Wildlife Service is ready in good faith to aid him in doing that."[1]

The settlement was considered a moral victory for Lin, but he still cannot till, plant, or water his land. He must submit an application to the FWS for permission to farm. He was also required to pay $5,000 restitution to the private Center for Natural Lands Man-

---

1. Letter to the editor, *The Sacramento Bee,* 21 May 1995.

agement. The money conserves habitat for endangered species in Kern County (more on this legal extortion in later chapters).

THE STEPHENS KANGAROO RAT

The Domenigoni family has owned their 3,200-acre ranch in western Riverside County, California, for five generations. They grow wheat, oats, and barley. For those unfamiliar with farming, standard agricultural practice is to leave a portion of land unplanted, or fallow, for a year so that the soil has a chance to rejuvenate, thereby keeping the land in good condition and increasing yields. The fallow ground also provides a home for wildlife—with whom the Domenigonis have been living in harmony for decades. The county itself has been very hospitable to wildlife. The Riverside County Habitat Conservation Agency buys habitat with the money from a $1,950-per-acre fee assessed to developers.[2]

In 1990, the Domenigonis discovered trespassing biologists surveying the fallow land on their ranch. The illegally acquired data was forwarded to FWS. The biologists found a population of Stephens kangaroo rats on the Domenigoni farm (a different subspecies from the Tipton kangaroo rat discussed above). The FWS prohibited the Domenigonis from plowing 800 fallow acres so that the rodents could be studied. It took the rats *three* years to traverse the Domenigoni property. When the FWS lifted the ban on planting, the Domenigonis were out about $400,000 in lost income and expenses for attorneys and biologists. The Domenigonis now plant every acre every year, reducing the land's yield, and eliminating all natural habitat for wildlife—in the fear that the rat will return and the use of their land taken from them.

When wildfires struck Southern California in 1993, twenty-

2. *Riverside Press,* 1 April 1995.

nine families in Riverside County lost their homes. They were pre-vented from digging firebreaks, a procedure known as discing, to keep their homes safe. Why? Because discing, according to the FWS, would disturb the burrows of Stephens kangaroo rats. Ranch owner Michael Rowe had been applying for a year for permission to disc his property. The Riverside fire department was urging people to disc their property. But FWS refused those requests. One night, Rowe smelled smoke in the air and saw fire roar in the nearby hills. Rowe went out and violated federal law by discing the land around his home.

Rancher Yshmael Garcia was the type of property owner the FWS likes. He obeyed the law and didn't disc his property. The rats were not disturbed—at least, not until the fire arrived. Rowe's house was saved and Garcia's burned to the ground. "My home was destroyed by a bunch of bureaucrats in suits and so-called environ-mentalists who say animals are more important than people," Gar-cia protested. "The only way to protect against fire is to build a firebreak, and we weren't allowed to do that." The fire, it should be mentioned, also destroyed the rats' burrows and probably many rats as well.

THE FAIRY SHRIMP

In September 1994, three species of fairy shrimp were designated as endangered, while a fourth was added to the threatened list. These crustaceans measure just over a half-inch in length and exist by the multitudes in California's Central Valley. One can find fairy shrimp almost everywhere—in ponds, pits, ditches, tire ruts, and "vernal pools." For those unfamiliar with the language of environ-mentalists, a "vernal pool" may be better known to you as a "mud puddle." They are depressions in the ground that are wet in the rain and dry in the sun. In fact, fairy shrimp are so prevalent that one is bound to disturb their habitat just about anywhere in the state. How can such a creature deserve federal protection? The story is even worse upon second glance. The *Wall Street Journal* obtained the listing documentation and discovered that the "federal listing decision was taken in response to a one-paragraph petition submitted by a Davis, California, botanist in 1990." The claim that fairy shrimp habitat was "imperiled" was based on nothing more than a "1978 paper written by a graduate student in botany who now admits he could not substantiate the study's conclusions."[3]

Confronted with these findings, an FWS Habitat Conservation Plan coordinator replied, "The incidental number of fairy shrimp found in puddles doesn't qualify as a viable population."[4]

These examples are taken from just one part of one state. We could go on to talk about Ben Cone of Pender County, North Carolina, and the red-cockaded woodpecker, or the timber workers of the Pacific Northwest and the spotted owl, or our experiences with the San Joaquin kit fox, which may not be an endangered species at all, but the product of breeding between an endangered species and unlisted species.

The California Biodiversity Alliance calls such experiences "governance by anecdote." Brian Vincent of the Greater Ecosystem Alliance in Bellingham, Washington, echoes the party line by complaining of an effort "to legislate by anecdote."[5] That's the standard attitude among many environmental groups—the ruination of the lives and livelihoods of ordinary citizens are simply *anecdotes*.[6] Representative Bruce Vento (D-Minnesota) calls them "cockamamie stories." A San Bernardino environmental activist called them "government by bumper sticker."

---

3. *The Wall Street Journal*, 21 October 1994.
4. "Tiny shrimp prompts giant questions," *The Grapevine Independent*, 19 April 1995.
5. "No scarcity of opinions," *The Columbian*, 23 April 1995.
6. Undated California Biodiversity Alliance press release.

Sometimes it is difficult to find environmentalists who think there is anything wrong with the Endangered Species Act. Or there are those like Zeke Grader, executive director of the Pacific Coast Federation of Fishermen's Associations, who say: "[ESA's] flaws lie in the fact that it is too weak, not too strong."[7] Journalists are not much better. Writing about the controversy, Charles McCoy, staff reporter of the *Wall Street Journal,* called the takings clause "a snippet of the Fifth Amendment."[8] I imagine he would object to "freedom of the press" referred to as "a snippet of the First Amendment."

MYTHS ABOUT THE ESA

Arguments in favor of the current Endangered Species Act and against compensation for regulatory takings run the gamut from moral to economic. What these arguments all share are serious flaws and an almost religious zeal—not for species, but for the act itself. What they are all missing is hard evidence to back up their claims. Their arguments can be categorized this way:

1. Landowners who benefit from public action should not be compensated when public action causes them a loss. Jerold S. Kayden, a Harvard University property rights scholar, has written: "Why shouldn't they have to repay the public when regulatory action—flood control, for example—enhances property values?"[9] This concept is seconded by Lee Talbot, the former senior scientist for the President's Council on Environmental Quality who helped write the ESA. Simple. First, unlike compensation for property taken, there is no provision in the Constitution for charging landowners for extra public

7. *The Fishermen's News,* January 1995.
8. Charles McCoy, "The Push to Expand Property Rights Stirs Both Hopes and Fears," *The Wall Street Journal,* 4 April 1995.
9. Ibid.

benefits and second, property owners already pay many times over for regulatory actions that may enhance property values—these payments are called *taxes*. If a landowner's income and property taxes are not paying for flood control or firefighting or roads, what are they for? Mr. Kayden should abdicate his "property rights scholar" title.

2. *Species are becoming extinct at a catastrophic rate*. In the 1980 Global 2000 Report to the President, Thomas Lovejoy wrote: ". . . of the 3 to 10 million species now present on the earth, at least 500,000 to 600,000 will be extinguished during the next two decades." The World Wildlife Fund raises funds with the claim: "Without firing a shot, we may kill one-fifth of all species of life on this planet in the next ten years." Environmentalists have been using these numbers for fifteen years. What they have not mentioned is that it is an extrapolation of a *guess* and has no scientific basis. For people who are so quick to decry anecdotal evidence, it is shocking to find that their "scientific" projections for species extinction are entirely anecdotal. It is futile to try to estimate future extinctions with any exactitude. For one thing, biologists cannot agree on what constitutes a species. Some maintain that there are seventy-four different species of grizzly bear.

Lovejoy's numbers were based entirely on a single reference, Norman Myers's book of 1979, *The Sinking Ark*. Myers estimated that the extinction rate of known species was one every four years between the years 1600 and 1900. From 1900 to 1980, he estimated the rate at one per year. From there, Myers claimed a spot extinction rate for 1980 at one hundred species per year. This hundredfold increase was based on a single staff-written news report in *Science* magazine citing "some scientists." The *Science* report also noted that this was not a spot extinction rate, but an upper limit. Using the geometric progression that has brought so many overpopulation activists to grief over the past 300 years, Lovejoy came up with his 40,000 extinctions per year by 2000. It is, quite clearly, hogwash passed off as science.

3. The act contributes to biodiversity. The Endangered Species Act has led to projects to "reintroduce" wildlife into areas where they were normally plentiful. These projects are often opposed by humans in the reintroduction area, since these species are often pests or predators. The U.S. Government's efforts in this regard have not been promising. Twelve black-footed ferrets were reintroduced into the Charles M. Russell National Wildlife Refuge in Montana. Three were eaten by coyotes within a week. But the coyotes couldn't gloat over their easy pickings. Gray wolves reintroduced into Yellowstone National Park are eating coyotes in the area. California condors, brought up in captivity and released into the "wild," have been found begging from humans outside fast-food restaurants. Residents of Willits, California, are concerned about what will happen when their local garbage dump is shut down. The dump is "habitat" and the source of all food for dozens of black bears. These bears simply could not survive in the wild.

4. The act has rescued many species from certain extinction. Environmental and wildlife literature abounds with tales of the ESA rescuing the alligator, gray whale, and bald eagle from extinction. In fact, of the more than 1,400 plant and animal species on the endangered or threatened list only twenty-seven species have been "de-listed"—and many of these de-listings were due to the species being miscounted in the first place.

Three endangered bird species on the Micronesian island of Palau were "recovered" when biologists found more birds. In 1973, there were 734,000 alligators—a number that indicates it was far from being endangered. Even the National Wildlife Federation admitted that "It now appears that the animal should never have been placed on the Endangered Species List."[10] The gray whale was never

---

10. Cited in *National Wilderness Institute Resource,* Vol. 5, Issue 1, Fall 1994.

officially declared a recovered species, but act supporters often cite it as a success. But the whale's population had been improving for over a century, tripling from fewer than 5,000 to about 14,000 three years before the act was approved. The whale owes its recovery to millionaire John D. Rockefeller, who persuaded Americans to use kerosene instead of whale oil for fuel.

5. *The FWS uses the best available data to make listings.* As illustrated in the Delhi Sands Flower Loving Fly case, it is possible for FWS to use the "best available data," but only if someone sends it to them. For fish and wildlife experts, FWS officials tend to accept a lot of claims at face value. The Mexican duck, for example, was granted federal protection. As a result, the Vaca family ranch in Arizona lost 200 acres from its grazing permit. Later it was discovered that there is no such thing as a Mexican duck. The birds in the area were mallards—perfectly common. The FWS removed the duck from the list.

Fish and Wildlife officials wanted to list the Alabama sturgeon as an endangered species. Fearing the economic implications to his state, Senator Richard Shelby (R-Alabama) demanded further study. When they finally examined the fish, they discovered it was genetically identical to the abundant Mississippi shovelnose sturgeon. The FWS aborted the listing petition.

The act must clearly define what is meant by the term "best available scientific and commercial data." Not all data is relevant. Not all data rises even to the lowest threshold of being evidence. Data claimed to be scientific must be derived from the use of generally recognized and accepted scientific methods and protocols. Blind peer review should be instituted to review all data and analyses. Qualified experts should be retained and should have no financial ties to FWS. The blind peer review should be published so that it is available to the public.

6. *Endangered species have medicinal values and may be the cure for cancer or AIDS.* While it is true that many of our most effective medicines and treatments come from plants, the claims of act support-

ers are hyperbolized beyond any supportable data. "The Endangered Species Act keeps us healthy," asserts a report from the Endangered Species Coalition, "by safeguarding many of the species upon which we rely for life-saving medicines to fight cancer and other life-threatening diseases. It protects yet undiscovered cures for diseases like AIDS."

The report then cites the discovery of a compound—Calanolide A—that "has proven to be 100 percent effective in preventing the replication of HIV-1." The compound came from a tree in a Malaysian swamp. When collectors returned to the site, the tree was gone and no similar tree could be found. This story was told at an environmental symposium in Nigeria in 1993. Its veracity is problematic, but even if true, the U.S. Endangered Species Act does not cover Malaysia. The economy of Malaysia does not allow for the kinds of private conservation efforts that are plentiful in the United States.

The U.S. Endangered Species Act could not have saved that tree.

The report mentions that the rosy periwinkle treats childhood leukemia and Hodgkin's disease. "This plant is native to a seriously endangered habitat in Madagascar," the report says. Again, Madagascar is a Third World nation concerned with feeding its citizens, not saving the rosy periwinkle. The U.S. Endangered Species Act cannot save the rosy periwinkle in Madagascar.

The report mentions *one* medicine from the United States. The drug taxol, described as "one of the most promising new treatments for ovarian and breast cancer," comes from the bark of the Pacific yew tree, found *primarily* in the Pacific Northwest. "The Pacific yew is native to an endangered ecosystem," the report states. *The Pacific yew is not an endangered species.* When the Endangered Species Coalition mentions "an endangered ecosystem," it means the Pacific Northwest! What is an ecosystem, you ask? An ecosystem defies conventional definition because no one can decide where one ends and another begins, what is present or what is absent, or anything else. It is an eco-buzzword that means "place." The U.S. Endangered Species Act cannot save the Pacific yew because the Pacific yew is not endangered.

So much for the medicinal value of endangered species. Notice that supporters of the current ESA never speculate that some of these species may carry organisms or bacteria that could be extremely harmful to humans or other life. Maybe their extinction will save us! The Ebola virus, with a mortality rate between 70 and 90 percent, is believed to have been first transmitted by monkeys in the Sudanese and Zairean rain forests. There is no vaccine or cure for Ebola hemorrhagic fever, which is ranked third among the deadliest infectious diseases (behind HIV and rabies). While no one is advocating the deliberate extinction of species, the fact that there may be dangers as well as "miracle cures" among endangered species points out the flaws in the environmentalist argument.

The medicinal value of plants is inarguable. We all benefit from it. So why should a few farmers and ranchers bear the costs of something than can benefit the whole world? Paul Campos, general counsel for the Building Industry Association of Northern California, summed it up best: "The more someone beats me over the head with the notion that the cure for cancer is in one these endangered plants . . . I say, 'Gosh, doesn't that make it even less fair for society to foist (the cost of preservation) on the few?' "[11]

---

11. Nancy Vogel, "Species act is facing its toughest test," *The Sacramento Bee,* 21 May 1995.

4

SWAMPED BY WETLANDS

"Ecologically speaking, the term 'wetland' has no meaning. For regulatory purposes, a wetland is whatever we decide it is."

—ROBERT J. PIERCE, U.S. ARMY CORPS OF ENGINEERS

They were once "the cause of malarial and malignant fevers" according to a turn-of-the-century Supreme Court ruling, which also asserted that "the police power is never more legitimately exercised that in removing such nuisances." The dictionary refers to them as "wet, spongy lands that are permanently or periodically covered with water." For centuries they have been known by the name "swamps." But today, they are called wetlands, and there are few limits on what government will do to "protect" them. A horde of confusing statutes gives joint jurisdiction over the nation's wetlands to the Environmental Protection Agency and the U.S. Army Corps of Engineers. How the EPA and the corps came to hold such awesome power should be a lesson in humility for any crusading lawmaker who thinks his or her bill will accomplish nothing more or less than what its language specifies.

The first link in the chain to "swamp feudalism" was the Federal Water Pollution Control Act of 1965, Section 404 of which sought to prevent pollution by requiring a permit to place dredge material in "navigable waters." The term "navigable waters" is defined in section 502 of the act as "waters of the United States, including the territorial seas." It was amended in 1972 (and renamed the Clean Water Act) to allow the federal government to regulate the discharge of pollutants into waters that *eventually* flowed into navigable waterways. There was never any mention of wetlands in Section 404, nor has the Congress authorized any regulation of wetlands since.

In 1975 the corps adopted a regulation defining the "waters of the United States" to include not only navigable waters but also their tributaries, interstate waters, and their tributaries, and non-navigable intrastate waters that affect interstate commerce. They also construed the term to include all freshwater wetlands adjacent to these waters. At that time, the corps defined wetlands as "areas periodically inundated and normally characterized by the prevalence of vegetation that requires saturated conditions for growth and reproduction." In 1977, the corps deleted the requirement of periodic inundation. The current definition provides that, "The term 'wetlands' means those areas that are inundated or saturated by surface or ground water at a frequency and duration sufficient to support, and that under normal conditions do support, a prevalence of vegetation typically adapted for life in saturated soil conditions. Wetlands generally include swamps, marshes, bog and similar areas."

In 1979, U.S. Attorney General Benjamin Civiletti ruled that the EPA—not the corps—had the ultimate authority to decide the limits of "waters of the United States." At that point, the corps stopped using the term "navigable" as the limit to its jurisdiction and started using "waters of the United States."

When the courts found these maneuvers to be overreaching, the

EPA and corps ignored them. In the 1982 case *U.S. v. Brassey,* the U.S. District Court in Idaho ruled that wetlands could not be regulated under the Clean Water Act unless they were recognizable by the "ordinary person" as a "normally aquatic environment." This eminently sensible decision changed nothing in federal procedures.

By 1985 the EPA had extended the Clean Water Act's coverage to millions of acres of *isolated* wetlands. EPA's rationale for regulating such prairie potholes and intermittently wet dry lands was that they were actual or potential habitat for migratory birds or endangered species. In 1985, the U.S. Senate Environment and Public Works Committee held oversight hearings on Section 404. During these hearings Senate Majority Leader Senator George Mitchell (D-Maine) called on the corps to enforce regulations of any waters "which are or could be used" by migratory birds which cross state lines. The idea was that when migratory birds cross state lines *they have an effect on interstate commerce and therefore can be regulated constitutionally under the Commerce Clause.* This incredible federal overreach was dubbed "the glancing goose test" because any land that a goose or duck might glance at—but not necessarily descend upon—could be regulated by the Corps of Engineers.

The delineation of wetlands continued to expand. The 1987 edition of the Corps of Engineers Manual defined them as "An area may have inundation or saturation (within 12 inches of surface) anywhere from 5 percent to 12 ½ percent of growing season (roughly 8 ½ to 21 days—15 days is average)." In other words, ground that was saturated within a foot of the surface less than nine days out the year was a "wetland."

But even that was not enough for the corps' regulation writers. The 1989 manual defined wetlands as areas that have water within eighteen inches of the surface for seven days during the growing season. The General Accounting Office noted that the corps was "significantly expanding the definition of the nation's wetlands." Some estimates indicate that the 1989 manual almost doubled the regulated area to 200 million acres—almost 40 percent of which was private land.

The Clean Water Act expired in 1992, but Congress has continued to fund it each year without bothering to reauthorize it. But the ultimate insult to American citizens occurred on 24 August 1993. That's when the Clinton administration's Interagency Working Group on Wetlands released a report recommending that "Congress should amend the Clean Water Act to make it consistent with the agencies' rulemaking." That is, of course, exactly the opposite of the way representative government is supposed to work. Congress writes the laws, the president signs them, and the bureaucracy carries them out. We cannot allow the bureaucratic tail to wag the dog.

The following stories will illustrate not only how property rights are routinely violated by Section 404 of the Clean Water Act, but how financial ruin can easily follow. Landowners are financially liable for removing unauthorized work and restoration of the wetland, and can be fined up to $50,000 per day for each violation. In extreme cases, violators can be sentenced up to three years in prison. If you avoid violating the Clean Water Act, you are still not out of the woods—or swamps. Landowners are often forbidden to use their land in any productive way, yet they are still charged normal property taxes on it. So, not only are these farmers and ranchers forced to forego any profit off their land, but they are charged for the privilege of having a federally protected swamp on their property.

If Congressmen cannot get the EPA and the Corps of Engineers to bend, what chance does the average American landowner have? None. Here are the stories of just a few of them:

JOHN PIAZZA

"The IRS is a walk in the park compared to the Corps," said John Piazza, describing the U.S. Army Corps of Engineers. Piazza is the president of the Piazza Construction Company in Mount Vernon, Washington. In 1991, the local government gave him a permit to build a ministorage facility on his land. But before he could begin construction, he was notified that portions of his land were wetlands. They were in three sections and totaled less than an acre. Piazza designed his facility so it would affect 0.18 of an acre of wetlands, and then he applied for an exemption.

The corps visited the site and determined that Piazza would have to conduct an extensive analysis of alternatives, an updated site plan, a mitigation plan, and consultation with two other federal agencies, along with public notice and comment. While waiting for this permit, a new definition of wetland was adopted by the corps and Piazza's wetlands actually shrank to 0.089 of an acre. Still, the corps would not grant an exemption. Piazza ended up spending more than $25,000 to preserve his "wetlands."

During his three-year wait for a permit, Piazza gave a senator a tour of his property in an attempt to explain his problem. At one point during the tour, the senator asked how long it would take them to get to the wetland. Mr. Piazza replied, "You're standing in it."[1]

WAYNE SCHELL

Wayne Schell owns a seventy-acre private nudist resort southeast of Sacramento, California. In 1987, Mr. Schell planned to expand his resort and wanted to widen an existing man-made lake from eight acres to more than twenty-seven acres. According to Schell, the new lake provides habitat for "25,000 fish, 2,000 bullfrogs, 100 wild ducks, 8 geese, 4 blue herons and 6 white herons." The corps said

---

1. "The Regulatory Quagmire of Wetlands Policy," by Jonathan Tolman, *The Competitive Enterprise Institute's Property Rights Reader,* January 1995.

that Schell's new lake had expanded into a wetland. Even though Schell was essentially creating a permanent wetland from a temporary one, the corps told him he needed to apply for a permit. Schell did, and the corps turned it down. In fact, it demanded that he remove the dam he had built for his expanded lake.

The corps claimed that the nearby Cosumnes River could conceivably flood over the top of the dam when salmon are spawning and thereby trap the salmon in the lake. This would be a remarkable occurrence if it ever happened, because no one has sighted a salmon in the Cosumnes River for over thirty years.

JAY COLVIN

Jay Colvin is the owner and operator of Colvin Farms in the little town of Eden, Arizona. His story:

"My personal problems started after the January 1992 flood. The little community of Eden is located on the north side of the Gila River. When the river runs over 150,000 cubic feet per second, Eden is cut off from the rest of the world. Not only was the river raging that January, but generally dry Markam Creek was overflowing. The 1992 flood was going over the top of the bridge, washing out the dikes that were part of a flood control project. This bridge is the only way out in case of emergency for the community of Eden during these high flows.

"The water broke through the dikes, heading directly for a wheelchair-bound resident's home. She had lived in that house for over 70 years. The house was made of adobe and it started to melt when the waters began running against it. The water then dumped into the canal, filling it up over flood stage, threatening the other homes in the area. It was also going through prime farmland, threatening to change the course of the creek.

"Something had to be done; the flood water was a threat to life and property. The creek lowered between storms enough to enable repairs of the existing dike. We saved her house, the canal, the fields, and the community of Eden. We did it without the help of the National Guard; we did it without the help of the county, state or federal agencies. And what did we receive for our good work? A threat of a felony because we disturbed a stream of the United States. We were accused of affecting the critical habitat of the river that was flowing at 175,000 cubic feet per second. We were accused of destroying fragile habitat in the stream bed that was made up of one-, two- and three-foot boulders. It was pointed out that we could be stirring up the turbidity of the river that was chocolate brown from all the farms being washed away at a rate of 175,000 cubic feet per second.

"I had been trying to get the Corps of Engineers down to help with our problems in the area. I was told they were the only ones that might help since it was a critical habitat area. When the representative of the corps showed up, I was eating dinner with the other farmers at the Pima Tastee Freeze. I thanked him for coming and said, let's go look at the devastation, and told him some ideas that I had. In front of all those farmers, he said, 'Sir, you do not understand. I am from the green side of the corps. We are not here to help, but to stop you from doing anything. In fact, we may charge you with a felony for your actions.' "[2]

2. Testimony before the Private Property Task Force, Phoenix, Arizona, 3 June 1995.

THE GERBAZ BROTHERS

In Carbondale, Colorado, the corps issued a permit to a neighbor of Dennis and Nile Gerbaz to repair damage caused by a 1984 flood on the Roaring Fork River. The neighbor lived upstream from the Gerbaz brothers and his repair work plus another flood event in 1985 caused flooding of five acres of the Gerbaz ranch. The land was rendered unusable by erosion and debris. The brothers requested a permit from the corps to repair the damage done to their ranch. Not only did the corps refuse a permit, but it refused even to send inspectors to look at the damage.

The Gerbazes' attorney told them there was a clause in the Clean Water Act that would allow them to restore their property and to put the river back into its original channel. They did the necessary work. That's when they received a summons to federal court and a fine of over $43 million. The Gerbazes have since spent more than $55,000 in legal costs, have been ordered by the federal government to devise a "river modification plan" at a projected cost of $150,000, and have seen their fines grow to over $51 million. The case is still in the courts. We need to ask if flood repair is now such an egregious offense that it calls for a fine of more than $50 million.[3]

LARRY FORE

Larry Fore of Latta, South Carolina, had farmed around an old tobacco-curing barn for twenty-five years. The barn covered a spot twenty feet wide and thirty feet long. It was crumbling and growing over with briars. Fore tore down the structure so that it would not interfere with his plowing and reported his action to the Agri-

---

3. Ibid.

cultural Stabilization and Conservation Service. Only then did he learn that the precise spot where the barn had sat was classified as a wetland. The area had never been wet, and no one would have built a tobacco-curing barn on a spot that was. This did not stop the federal swamp protectors. A provision in the Food Security Act of 1985 allows the federal government to deny farm program benefits if an otherwise eligible farmer alters a wetland. So now Larry Fore farms around a twenty-by-thirty-foot rectangle of useless ground in the middle of his field.[4]

OCIE MILLS

In January 1989, Ocie Mills and his son Carey of Navarre, Florida, were convicted of "four felony counts of knowingly discharging fill material in wetlands, one misdemeanor count for willfully discharging fill material in wetlands, and one misdemeanor count of dredging a canal in navigable waters." They were sentenced to twenty-one months in a federal penitentiary and $5,000 fines each for putting nineteen loads of clean sand on their less than half-acre lot of dry, residentially zoned parcel of land. The fill had been approved by the state of Florida. The "canal" they dredged was actually an existing 300-foot drainage ditch. Mills had cleaned it out to improve drainage and control mosquitoes.

Why were Mills and his son convicted of felonies? This letter from U.S. Army Corps District Colonel Charles T. Myers III to the U.S. Attorney gave some clues: "Due to Mr. Mills's highly publicized prior involvement with the Corps Regulatory Program . . . , his documented furnishing of advice to others with intent to subvert the Corps Regulatory Program . . . , it is recommended that Mr. Mills be prosecuted criminally."

---

4. Ibid.

U.S. District Judge Roger Vinson, reviewing the Mills case in 1993, wrote: "This case presents the disturbing implications of the expansive jurisdiction which has been assumed by the U.S. Army Corps of Engineers under the Clean Water Act. In a reversal of terms that is worthy of *Alice in Wonderland,* the regulatory Hydra which emerged from the Clean Water Act mandates in this case that a landowner who placed clean fill dirt on a plot of subdivided dry *land* may be imprisoned for the statutory felony offense of 'discharging pollutants into the navigable *waters* of the United States.'" [emphasis in original]

FRED AND NANCY CLINE

Nancy Cline of Sonoma, California, appeared before the House Committee on Resources Task Force on Wetlands, on 19 April 1995. Here is her story in her own words:

> I am Nancy Cline, mother of five young children, owner of a small family winery in Sonoma, California, and member of The Fairness to Land Owners Committee.
>
> I am here today to urge you to swiftly pass legislation to ensure the equal protection of the private property rights of those who can't afford to spend their life savings fighting the unchecked power of the federal bureaucrats.
>
> I am here today to expose the nightmare we have been living.
>
> For the last several years the bureaucrats have threatened us and intimidated us into silence. Speaking today, I risk further retaliation by the bureaucrats against my precious family. However, after a great deal of soul searching, my husband and I decided that the government has already shattered our dreams, devastated our family, threatened

our financial security and diminished our respect for our government. We also came to the stark reality that if we can be intimidated into silence then the future of our precious children is at great risk—for they will have no freedom in their future.

Early in 1989, my husband wanted to fulfill his life-long dream of creating and owning a family winery. My husband and I purchased 350 acres in Sonoma; it seemed the perfect place to raise our family, farm and establish a small winery.

Fred immediately began to farm the land. He worked hand in hand with the Soil Conservation Service, who indicated in August 1990 that the U.S. Army Corps of Engineers wanted to speak with him about his agricultural practices.

A corps official showed up at the property and informed Fred that he believed that the property was a wetland. Fred showed the agent that the government's aerial photo of our so-called wetlands was an overflowing watering trough for cattle.

Then the agent mentioned an endangered salt marsh harvest mouse.

The corps enforcement officer told Fred that plowing was OK, leveling was not. Leveling is the spreading of dirt to make a field easier to plant. This is a regular farming practice in our area.

Although Fred agreed to adhere to his orders, the agent went back to his office and issued an intimidating Cease and Desist Order saying that they 'discovered an unauthorized activity,' and threatened us with fines of up to $25,000 per day or imprisonment of up to a year.

It was the first time we had heard the term wetland to describe our land. It was the first time we heard that the federal government had jurisdiction over farming.

We hired an expert attorney on land use and the Clean

Water Act, who indicated that since our property had been grazed and farmed since 1930, Fred's farming activities were agriculturally exempt. Our attorney said he would write a letter and get the Cease and Desist Order rescinded.

Fred continued to plow and plant hay—told by both the Corps and our attorney that both these farming practices were fine.

Daily we expected the Cease and Desist Order to be rescinded.

I think back now, and wonder how we could have been so naive. My God, we had no idea that these people would try to destroy our family. We thought they would recognize the obvious agricultural history of our property and move on.

In December 1991, corps agents issued another Cease and Desist Order. We met at the property hoping for resolution but the agents insisted that the flapgate and the mere plowing of our hayfield constituted a violation of the Clean Water Act.

We spent thousands of dollars for our attorney to provide exhaustive documentation to the corps that the property was in agricultural use for the last 60 years and that virtually all of Fred's activities were ag-exempt and not regulated by the Clean Water Act or the corps regulations.

Again, our attorney assured us that our property and activities were exempt. Not to worry, the corps would see the light.

The corps responded that it didn't matter. They wanted the property put back the way it was before agricultural use.

In November 1992, a letter arrived from the corps. Despite the massive and expensive documentation provided by our attorney, we were told we had 45 days to close our flapgates, fill in any ag ditches, restore the site to its pre-agricultural state, post a bond for the corps to be assured of our intentions, and be prepared to hire an environmental consultant for five years to monitor the site according to the corps' wishes.

Obviously, continued farming was out of the question.

Throughout this time period, we requested many meetings with the corps to resolve this issue. They promised to meet yet they wouldn't. To date, and I mean as of February 1995, they have refused to meet with us or our attorney.

In January 1994, the FBI showed up. Obviously the corps had no desire to discuss or resolve this issue. We were told to hire a criminal attorney.

I don't know how to convey to you the terrifying and gut-wrenching experience of being the target of a criminal investigation. We sank into utter helplessness as we finally realized that they had no intention—and never had—of resolving our simple problem.

Their issue was power and control. Their issue was an edict from the U.S. Attorney General demanding more criminal environmental convictions in the Ninth Circuit—apparently short of the prescribed quotas.

The FBI and EPA interrogated neighbors, acquaintances and strangers. They asked about our religion, whether we were intelligent, did we have tempers. They asked how we treat our children.

Our property was surveyed by military helicopters. Their cars monitored our home and our children's school. They accused Fred of paying neighbors to lie. The FBI actually told one terrified neighbor that this investigation was top secret, with national security implications. The community reeled, as did we.

Our personal papers were subpoenaed. The grand jury was convened.

We spent thousands of additional dollars to hire more attorneys. The Justice Department told our attorneys that— unless we would plead guilty and surrender our land—they would seek a criminal indictment of both Fred and me. According to one government attorney, I was to be included because I had written a letter to the editor of a local paper, in their opinion "publicly undermining the authority of the Army Corps."

Let me tell you—it has been a wretched nightmare. A nightmare for my husband, a nightmare for my children and a nightmare for me. I will never be able to adequately express what this abuse of power, the threat of prison, the use of the FBI, and the intimidation used to get us to plead guilty did to our family this last year.

After months of anxiety, anger, sleepless nights, and $100,000 of legal fees, we decided that there was no way we were going to plead guilty when we were absolutely innocent of any criminal behavior.

I remind you that in the midst of this sinister lunacy, Fred and I had five tender children to nurture and protect. Our decision to stand up for our family, our children's legacy and future, and our dreams has cost us dearly—both emotionally and financially.

With us refusing to surrender, the agencies knew that they did not have a criminal—and, in our opinion, not even a civil—case. Two months ago, they informed our attorney—orally, of course—that they were not proceeding on criminal charges.

To date, the corps has refused to resolve the issue and rescind the Cease and Desist Orders. With these orders still in effect, half of our farm is restricted from participating in regular farming activity.

The agony of this experience has left deep scars.

We have no idea how to settle this issue or how to resolve the horrible wrenching pain of last year. We remain at the mercy of the bureaucrats and their next interpretation of their regulations. We are terrified that they might try to retaliate upon learning of my appearance here today.

We are not alone. Across this country the bureaucrats are abusing landowning citizens. The people are rightfully terrified to come forward. They are intimidated into silence.

I urge you to make these abusive federal agencies accountable to you. They are running amok in this country—destroying the dreams, financial and emotional security of decent, productive citizens.

They had no right to strip Fred and me of our dreams. They had no right to force us to spend our children's legacy to protect ourselves from incarceration; from prison.

This is not about protecting the environment. It's about agencies out of control and in need of adult supervision. This is about their desire and power to control land and their total disregard for private property rights. And it is about the future of this great country.

These agents have stolen our dreams and our land. If they want our land, I urge you to make them pay for it.

JOHN POZSGAI

John Pozsgai of Morristown, Pennsylvania, bought a dump next to a small stream bed. He removed tons of garbage, thousands of old tires and car parts, and replaced this public eyesore with clean dirt. He was charged and convicted of filling a wetland without a permit, and sentenced to 33 months in prison in 1991.[5]

BILL ELLEN

Bill Ellen of Mathews, Virginia, was hired to create a wildlife sanctuary, including ten duck ponds on a 3,200-acre property in Dorchester County, Maryland. He was charged and convicted of filling a wetland without a permit, sentenced to six months in prison, four months of home detention, one year of supervised release and a $100 fine. The EPA claimed that the ten wildlife ponds Bill created degraded the environment because ducks and geese would defecate in the ponds. This argument confused even the judge in the case. He asked the EPA expert witness: "Are you saying that there is pollution from ducks, from having waterfowl on a pond—that pollutes the water?"

> EPA WITNESS: "Your honor, when you concentrate a large number of ducks—"
> JUDGE: "Have you ever been on the Eastern Shore [of Maryland]?"
> EPA WITNESS: "Yes, your honor."
> JUDGE: "Aren't there a lot of freshwater ponds?"
> EPA WITNESS: "Yes, your honor."
> JUDGE: "And is it against the law to have ducks and geese on them?"
> EPA WITNESS: "No, your honor."

5. *News from the Floc,* June 1995.

Swamped by Wetlands

GASTON AND MONIQUE ROBERGE

In 1986, Gaston and Monique Roberge of Old Orchard, Maine, contracted to sell a lot they had held for over twenty years for $440,000 to fund their retirement. The corps claimed their land was a filled wetland and that all the dirt had to be removed. The Roberges had not placed the fill on the land. The town of Old Orchard had done so in 1976. It didn't matter to the corps. The sale of the Roberge's land fell through because of the corps attention and the value of the land plummeted. It took the Roberges eight years to win a corps admission that they never had jurisdiction over his land. In December 1994, the Justice Department settled with the Roberges for $338,000 after their lawyers uncovered a 1987 memo from corps' field agent Jay Clement to the regional chief of enforcement which said: "Roberge would be a good one to squash and set an example . . ." Clement signed his name to the memo and added "formerly the Maytag Repairman." Apparently "squashing" the Roberges (Gaston is eighty-two, Monique is seventy-two) was simply a way for the corps to combat boredom.

HOWARD AND GRACE HECK

Howard and Grace Heck's only asset is a twenty-five-acre parcel in Farmingdale, New Jersey, that they bought in the early 1970s to build modestly priced homes. That property is now worthless because in 1987 the corps claimed it was a "jurisdictional wetland." Grace is now seventy-eight with a history of strokes and cancer. Howard is eighty-three with a long history of heart disease. The property was once worth $2 million. Now they live on social security.

Bedridden, Howard wrote his story, and Grace read it to a Private Property Rights Roundtable in December 1994:

In October 1992—when the corps put our permit application out for public comment—they stated that our property was a "regulated palustrine forested broad-leaved deciduous wetland." It was just a dry and dense hardwood forest to me!

Responding to the corps, the U.S. Fish and Wildlife Service recommended denial of our permit because they said that there was a federally threatened plant species "within five miles of the proposed project site." No one will buy a parcel under this kind of bureaucratic control and we cannot afford an attorney to exercise our rights under the Constitution.

Sitting idly by, Congress has permitted very powerful bureaucrats to deny untold numbers of Americans their rights under the Fifth and Fourteenth Amendments. For when the government comes in and "takes" our land through unreasonable regulations—they take, in many cases, the only asset we have to defend our rights. And thus, we are denied the "equal protection under the law" as guaranteed by our forefathers.

So, as our once valuable land now sits as a free public park, while we are destitute and living with our daughter and her 12-year-old daughter in her two-bedroom home, while we struggle to exist on our monthly Social Security check, while we can no longer afford our family doctor of thirty years—a very discomforting situation with my health and the fact that Grace has had a stroke and breast cancer, while we both need hearing aids but can't afford them, while we are unable to have a social life because we can't afford to go out with our few friends who are still around, and while we have to skimp on other things just to get our teeth cleaned, the government has seized control of our life savings.

I assure you that it is not a dignified way to live and a severe blow to my pride. Our once secure and independent life has now become a nightmare. I feel like I'm mired in an awful mess and I can't find a way out. The isolation and humiliation is terrible.

Our government has not only stolen the land we worked hard to buy, but it has robbed us of the last seven years of our precious and short remaining time on earth. Our senior years—that we worked hard to be able to enjoy and be independent.

I have never asked our government for anything. We were proud to be Americans in a land where we and our children were to have the opportunity to achieve any goal we wanted. Now we are ashamed of our country and a government that allows the bureaucrats to steal from its citizens under the false pretense that it is for the public good.

I am asking our elected representatives to rein in the bureaucrats' power and their expansion of the regulatory stranglehold. And I am asking our government to buy and pay us for our land if they want to prevent us from using it or selling it. For if our land is so valuable that it cannot be developed, then it should be valuable enough for the public to own it!

When the Hecks and Clines appeared on Capitol Hill to tell their stories, Michael Bean of the Environmental Defense Fund told the *Bureau of National Affairs* newsletter: "[I]f those people can afford to fly to Washington for the forum, they can probably afford a lawyer." What's more, the EDF attempted to smear the Hecks and Clines by passing out a list of anonymous allegations against them. By mistake, the list was given to a staffer of Rep. Charles Canady (R-Florida), who discovered the identity of the group behind it.

RICHARD AND NANCY DELENE

Richard and Nancy Delene live in a log cabin and own 2,400 acres in Michigan's Upper Peninsula. The Delenes created twenty-six acres of ponds and enhanced over one hundred acres of habitat for all forms of wildlife on their property—all out of their own pockets and through their own hard work. At the time, Michigan was the only state authorized by the EPA to have full authority over its wetlands. The Delenes and the Michigan Department of Natural Resources (DNR) were locked in a dispute over the duck ponds for over a year. The DNR claimed that in creating the ponds the Delenes had polluted the Sturgeon River. The DNR and the State Attorney General charged Richard with moving dirt without permits. The Delenes were facing potential fines in excess of $1.2 million and were under permanent restraining order. They had obeyed a Stop Work injunction and all construction has ceased. The DNR had offered a settlement if the Delenes would grant the state a right-of-way, which was legal right to pass over the Delenes' property but they refused this offer.

On 14 December 1993, the Delenes were writing Christmas cards when a commotion began outside. Looking out the window, the Delenes saw two DNR trucks and a county sheriff's vehicle. Just to get on the land, the officials would have had to cut a padlock at the gate where the Delenes had posted a large sign saying LAND PATENTS PROTECT THIS LAND. NO TRESPASSING! The agents and the sheriffs called on the Delenes to open the door. "For about an hour, I wouldn't answer them as I was assessing what Nancy and I should do," said Richard. "We don't have a phone in the cabin and I couldn't call for help or call my attorney."

Shortly after the commotion started, Michigan state troopers arrived. "They were all armed!" Richard later described. "There were a bunch of high-powered rifles aimed at our cabin. I said to Nancy, 'What are we in for?' We saw at least three DNR guys, the deputy sheriff and about four or five state troopers."

There was a standoff. The Delenes refused to come out of their home to face armed troopers and the troopers would not put away their arms because Delene was known to have hunting rifles in the house (Delene did, but he never touched them during the incident). The five-hour siege was in danger of becoming the first environmental Waco when the Delenes' lawyer arrived. All the police and DNR officials left soon after. The state trooper who had been negotiating with the Delenes admitted, "I've been with the force for a while and I've never been on such a farce in my life!"

The compounded irony is that just six months before, the county had given Richard Delene the "Outstanding Agricultural Cooperator" award. A county official lauded Delene's environmental record: "He believed in wetlands well before it was fashionable. . . . He used his own land, equipment and money to develop . . . wildlife ponds."

Richard Delene believes he knows why the state decided to make an example of him: "Just 24 miles north of my site the state has spent over $2 million of taxpayers' money, with limited wildlife benefits, to create what I created with my own funds. They're draining swamps, bulldozing heaps of dead trees. One is not sure whether it's a moonscape or a parking lot under construction."[6]

YOUR TRAGEDY IS AN "ANECDOTE"

"Anecdotes" like these do not impress the environmental movement. Their "let them eat cake" attitude shows equal disdain for large corporations and individuals. The Koll Real Estate group wanted to build 3,300 homes in Bolsa Chica, California. In exchange for permission, the developer agreed to spend $48 million to restore all of the area's wetlands, except approximately 200 acres on which 900

---

6. "FLOC members under armed siege over duck ponds," *News from the FLOC,* February 1994.

of the homes would be built. To forestall the development, the federal government offered to buy the land for $17.5 million—37 percent of the property's appraised value. When Koll turned down this fire sale offer, environmentalists and politicians alike scolded them. "Who else is going to purchase these wetlands?" said Connie Boardman of the Bolsa Chica Land Trust. "When it suits them, they will sell." David Sullivan, a Huntington Beach city councilman, said, "I think Koll should consider themselves extremely lucky to get $17 million."

Ultimately, Koll sold the wetlands to a consortium of federal and state agencies for $24 million. The developers will build 2,400 homes on bluffs overlooking the wetlands. While none of the Bolsa Chica wetlands will be developed, taxpayers will now have to generate the $24 million for the purchase. Koll keeps the $48 million it was going to spend for wetland restoration, which will now have to be made up by the ports of Los Angeles and Long Beach.

Both environmentalists and federal agencies are fond of reporting that the Corps of Engineers denies only 10 percent of development permits. What they fail to mention are the vast majority of applications that are withdrawn by frustrated and flummoxed landowners. Bernard N. Goode, a former corps engineering consultant, and attorney Virginia S. Albrecht did a study of the corps' permit process:

- "It took the average applicant 373 days to get through the individual permit process;
- "93 percent of the individual permit applications exceeded the 60 day standard for 'evaluation time' specified in Corps regulations;
- "63 percent of the individual applications decided in 1992 and 56 percent of applications decided between 1988 and 1993 ended up being withdrawn by either the applicant or the Corps;

- "One-fourth of the 410 individual applications we reviewed from 1992 involved impacts to less than one-quarter acre of wetland and just under half of the 1992 applications involved impacts of less than one acre; and
- "During Fiscal Year 1993, the total acreage of wetlands impacts authorized through the Corps permitting program (including nationwide and regional general permits as well as individual permits) was 11,600 acres, for which the Corps required 15,200 acres of mitigation."

If you thought the federal government would be content with the 200 million acres currently regulated as wetlands, think again. The U.S. Fish and Wildlife Service has a North American Wetlands Conservation Council that provides grants to purchase wetlands in Canada and Mexico. The nine-member council recommends wetlands conservation proposals to the Migratory Bird Conservation Commission, which approves funding. At least 50 percent and not more than 70 percent of the funds have to be spent on projects in Canada and Mexico. "Grant requests should not exceed $1.5 million, except in extraordinary circumstances," the council tells us. If a grant request is for less than $500,000, federal officials are not even required to visit the site.

The message from the federal government about wetlands is constructed in such a way as to lead Americans to only one, state-approved option. Wetlands have extraordinary value. They are in danger of being eradicated by greedy developers. Said developers cannot be trusted to preserve the wetlands on their own. Ergo, the wetlands must be brought under the direct control of the "public." Private land, subject to the whims of private individuals, becomes "public land," ostensibly managed for the good of all. However, as with "interstate commerce," "just compensation," and "wetlands," the government has its own definition of "public land."

5

REMOVING THE PUBLIC
FROM PUBLIC LANDS

"[Land] should all be in the public domain. Be unreasonable.
You can do it. Let's take it all back."

—BROCK EVANS, AUDUBON SOCIETY LOBBYIST, SPEAKING AT
TUFTS UNIVERSITY IN 1990

The sorry state of private property rights in America should not distract us from the severe encroachments on *public* property rights. Just as the Constitution is no longer read for what it says, we no longer make any distinction between public lands and government lands. The word "public" means "of, belonging to, or concerning the people as a whole; of or by the community at large." The U.S. government owns huge tracts of land, but a great deal of it is for public use, that is, private citizens are still permitted to make economic use of the land. This is what is supposed to be meant by the term "public land." The U.S. government does need to own some land for its own use and, as usual, the Constitution describes exactly for what uses the government may purchase and utilize land. The Constitution gives Congress exclusive legislative authority "over all places purchased, by the consent of the legislature of the state in which the same shall be, for the erection of forts, magazines, arsenals, dockyards, and other needful buildings."

This clause of the Constitution, along with the provisions of the Northwest Ordinance of 1787, are the fuel of the "county supremacy," "equal footing," "states' rights," and "10th Amendment" movements. Controversies over the use of public lands form the basis of the "War on the West" complaints by westerners. All these movements are predicated on decentralizing or eliminating federal control of public lands. Easterners have not been fully aware of these movements because these issues do not greatly affect them. But the use of public lands is high on the list of concerns in the western states.

FEDERAL OWNERSHIP OF THE WEST

Statistics tell why. The U.S. government controls approximately 726 million acres (or one-third) of America's 2.315 billion acres. Most of this public land is located west of the Mississippi River. More than half of the land in the eleven westernmost states is federally administered. The U.S. government controls 86.1 percent of Nevada, 63.8 percent of Idaho, and 63.6 percent of Utah.

This puts western states at a clear fiscal and economic disadvantage because, of course, the Feds do not pay property taxes to states for these lands, which private property owners would. Property taxes generally fund public schools and local services. By holding all this land, the U.S. government virtually eliminates the tax base of local and state governments in the West.

Holdings of the Department of Defense make up a part of federally controlled land, but a growing percentage is set aside for wilderness purposes. While military bases tend to improve local

economies in the West, wildlife preserves tend to forestall economic activity. Four government agencies control the vast majority
of these wilderness areas: the U.S. Forest Service, the U.S. Fish and
Wildlife Service, the National Park Service, and the Bureau of Land
Management. While there is overlapping authority in some geographic locations, this data will illustrate the extent of federal land
control by the "wilderness" agencies.

- The U.S. Forest Service controls 191.5 million acres in
  forty-four states, Puerto Rico, and the Virgin Islands. The
  acreage consists of 156 individual forests plus twenty grass-
  land units. The Forest Service's budget for 1995 was $1.345
  billion.
- The U.S. Fish and Wildlife Service controls 87.4 million acres,
  almost all of which are in the western states. The acreage
  consists of 504 refuges. The budget of the Fish and Wildlife
  Service for 1995 was $219 million.
- The National Park Service runs about 77 million acres in forty-
  nine states, the District of Columbia, Puerto Rico, Virgin Islands, Guam, Samoa, and the Northern Marianas. The acreage
  consists of 368 national parks and other protected areas. The
  National Park Service's budget for 1995 was $1.079 billion.
- The Bureau of Land Management controls about 268 million
  acres, almost all of which are in the western states. This land
  is divided into fifty-nine districts, then subdivided into 137
  resource areas. The bureau's budget for 1995 was $598 mil-
  lion.

Environmental groups are fond of sending out fundraising letters
warning about the disappearing wilderness. This tactic works very
well in the urban areas of the Northeast, where cities are batched
side by side, and urban sprawl causes immense problems. But out

in the West, the idea that the wild is disappearing causes peals of laughter. People who see the state of California as San Diego, Los Angeles, and San Francisco with some stuff in between might be surprised to know that California's land is almost 50 percent controlled by the federal government and that 77 percent of that federal land is set aside in some type of permanent wildlife preserve, wild and scenic river, or other wilderness area.

"I have been lied to," remarked a colleague of mine upon his return from a recent trip to northern California. "I flew around for five hours in a small plane and never saw anything but trees." The environmental communities' claims of clear-cut and disappearing forests did not materialize. A former supporter of the "Big Green" agenda, this colleague is now a staunch opponent.

A study by the Pacific Research Institute revealed that urban areas use about 60 million acres of land in the continental United States—a mere 3.1 percent of the total land in the lower forty-eight states. The report concludes: "Urban and suburban use of land has been growing by about 1 million acres a year since the end of World War II. At this rate (which in fact is likely to decline in the coming decades), it will take 190 years for urban and suburban areas to cover 10 percent of the total land area in the continental United States. Meanwhile, the amount of land dedicated to parks and wilderness areas has been growing twice as fast as urban areas. Land dedicated to wildlife has tripled since 1949."[1]

Such huge holdings have not diminished the federal government's hunger for more territory. I received much criticism from environmental groups for opposing the establishment of the Stone Lakes Wildlife Refuge in California. In testimony before the House Committee on Resources in March 1995, farmer John

---

1. *The Index of Leading Environmental Indicators,* The Pacific Research Institute, December 1994.

Baranek explained how the federal government carries out its land grabbing.

We as landowners felt comfortable with the original 5,000-acre refuge in North Stone Lake, most of which was already under a combination of state and county public ownership. To our surprise, at a meeting of the Sacramento County Board of Supervisors, we were introduced to a 74,000-acre study area as a proposed refuge! We became irate, and were able to convince the Supervisors to require Fish and Wildlife to add two directors from local reclamation districts to the 'Group' membership. They were added to the 'Group,'which then never held another meeting!

Overwhelming public opposition forced Fish and Wildlife to reduce the 74,000-acre proposal to a 9,000-acre core area, with an additional 9,000-acre cooperative management area. . . . Throughout this process, the service has proclaimed they are not enemies of property owners, because of the policy of purchasing only from willing sellers. Mr. Chairman, 'willing seller' is a farce. It is a cruel hoax on landowners. It is part of the overall plan to bleed property owners dry, until they have no option but to sell, and no one to sell to except the New Lords of the Manor, the Fish and Wildlife Service.

When this refuge was created by the stroke of a pen from some bureaucrat in Portland, Oregon, property values of inholders became subject to reduced value, due to lack of demand for the property. No one in the farming community is interested in purchasing land that comes under the influence of Fish and Wildlife refuge regulations.

Mr. Chairman, the United States Fish and Wildlife Service is a two-faced, power-hungry bureaucracy bent on grabbing land however they can. If the staff is spread too thin, they will shortchange another program. If they face owners unwilling to sell, they cast a regulatory cloud over private property.

There is no need for federal bureaucrats, backed up by big city environmentalists, to 'save' Stone Lakes. My family and my neighbors are doing just fine living among the ducks and other wildlife, and have been for well over one hundred years.

State governments have taken their cue from the Feds and employed some of the same tactics. But while the federal government was seeking to buy more land, the California state government was finding ways to steal it. The California Coastal Commission acquired one hundred miles of scenic land on the California coast from private property owners without having to pay a dime. The commission would require landowners to dedicate portions of their property to the state in return for coastal permits. This practice was declared unconstitutional by the United States Supreme Court in 1987. The court ruled that the Commission was engaged in "an out and out plan of extortion."[2]

While these land grabs are virtually always for the professed purpose of conservation, they often serve less humanitarian concerns. The public expects its governments to purchase and utilize land for things providing a public benefit—like fire stations, schools, highways, and military bases. Government officials, on the other hand, sometimes buy land for their own benefit. It has been a common practice for governments to assemble small parcels of land for sale to large businesses, particularly when recalcitrant landowners refuse to sell their property. These landowners can be threatened with property condemnation or regulatory hell by government bureau-

---

2. *Nollan v. California Coastal Commission,* US Supreme Court 1987.

crats. Usually they sell. If not, the government condemns the property anyway.

THE DESERT PROTECTION ACT

The natural appetite of governments for private property expands exponentially when the possibility of political gain is added to the mix. The history of the Desert Protection Act is illustrative. First proposed in 1986 by Senator Alan Cranston (D-California), the act established 7.75 million acres of protected wilderness in the California desert, an area the size of the state of Maryland, including the two new national parks of East Mojave and Death Valley. For eight years, the bill could make no headway in Congress. Reintroduced by Senator Dianne Feinstein (D-California), the bill was signed into law by President Clinton in October 1994. One of the bill's stated purposes is to preserve the historical and cultural values of the desert, including those associated with "patterns of western exploration and settlement, and sites exemplifying the mining, ranching and railroading history of the Old West." The bill does this by, what else, banning exploration, settlement, mining, ranching, and railroading.

The bill had "sprung from the brow" of the Sierra Club, one of the largest and wealthiest environmental organizations in the United States. The wilderness designation acreage figures (some say the maps themselves) came straight from its directors. The Sierra Club's interest in the Desert Protection Act was matched by the agents and shareholders of the Catellus Corporation. Catellus, at the time a subsidiary of Sante Fe Pacific Railroad, is a developer of commercial real estate. Its largest shareholder is the California Public Employees' Retirement System. The firm owns over 350,000 acres in the desert, land that was designated protected wilderness by the Desert Protection Act. The firm gives generously to many California politicians, including more than $100,000 to Senator Dianne Feinstein, the sponsor of the act.[3]

Because Catellus's nearly worthless desert acreage would be "taken" as wilderness, the federal government was required to pay them compensation. Coincidentally or not, Catellus was featured prominently in the original version of the bill introduced by Senator Feinstein. The original language stated: "Upon request of the Catellus Development Corporation, the Secretary [of the Interior] shall enter into negotiations for an agreement or agreements to exchange Federal lands or interests." Six months after the act passed, the secretary was to give Catellus a list of lands for exchange, with the first priority of "lands, including lands with mineral and geothermal interests, which have the potential for commercial development but which are not currently under lease or producing revenues." If the Feds could not come up with suitable land to exchange by October 1996, they would have to buy Catellus's land immediately, and the money could be credited to Catellus if it desired to *buy* U.S. land it desired.

This arrangement sent up warning flares on Capitol Hill, because the arrangement would move Catellus to the head of the line, while others would have to wait out lengthy compensation procedures. "Some property owners are more equal than others," said Chuck Cushman of the American Land Rights Association. Only after much effort and procedural maneuvering were congressional Republicans able to get this provision dropped from the final bill. Why Catellus had to receive its swap first became clear when one considered the lack of federal land available for trading in California.

As mentioned earlier, most of the federally owned land in California is protected wilderness. The architects of the Desert Pro-

---

3. "An Economic Desert," *The Orange County Register*, 25 September 1994. Editorial cites *San Francisco Chronicle* as source of figure.

tection Act were not about to trade wilderness for wilderness. The idea is to control *more* wilderness. The only other land the Bureau of Land Management had available to swap was decommissioned military bases. One of the potential sites was the Chocolate Mountain Aerial Gunnery Range. Coincidentally or not, the land just south of the range's southern fence is also owned by Santa Fe Pacific—more specifically, it is the Mesquite Gold Mine, one of the top ten mines in the United States. Engineers who have worked at the Mesquite mine think the vein runs north into the gunnery range, and Bureau of Land Management surveys seem to bear them out. "The real gusto is past the wire," as one engineer put it.

The range could contain gold deposits worth over $100 billion. "This range of mountains is currently one of the hottest gold exploration targets on the North American continent," said Don Fife, former interior secretary advisor for the California Desert Conservation Area.

The list of available land, which was due within six months of passage of the Desert Protection Act, did not appear for more than a year. Two half-sections (about 600 acres) of the Chocolate Mountain Aerial Gunnery Range have been handed over to the Bureau of Land Management. The Bureau can now use this acreage to compensate Catellus. The half-sections just happen to be adjacent to the Mesquite mines and, in the words of one Resource Committee expert, "are considered highly speculative (there's gold in them there half-sections)."

Besides this sweetheart deal, the act contained the usual pork. It created the fifteen-member Mojave National Park Advisory Commission (expenses paid by taxpayers) and funded a study to find lands suitable for a reservation in Death Valley National Park for the Timbisha Shoshone tribe (if the Shoshone could live there without damaging the environment, why shut others out?) At the time, the chairman of the Senate Energy and Natural Resources Committee was Senator J. Bennett Johnston (D-Louisiana). So it is not surprising to find that the Desert Protection Act establishes a Center for Excellence in the Sciences at Alcorn State University in Mississippi, in cooperation with Southern University in Baton Rouge, Louisiana; a Center for Aquaculture Studies at the University of Arkansas at Pine Bluff, also in cooperation with Southern University in Baton Rouge, Louisiana; "infrastructure facilities" at minority universities in the Mississippi Delta Region; a Delta Region Native American Cultural Center; a Delta Region African American Cultural Center; planning grants for minority and rural museums in the Delta Region (this one contains a legislative Freudian slip when, instead of funding all forms of "expressive culture," the bills refers to all forms of "expensive culture"); the New Orleans Jazz Historical Park (land acquisition approved); the seventeen-member New Orleans Jazz Commission (with per diem, travel expenses, equipment, and facilities); and a Music Heritage Program "with specific emphasis on the Mississippi Delta Blues."

This monstrous law created the single largest withdrawal ever of federal land from public use in the continental United States. All told, the California Desert produces $1.6 billion in mineral extraction per year. New mining is now forbidden by the act. The appropriation of private property removes $63 million in state tax revenues. The Interior Department estimated that new desert park facilities and operations would cost an additional $36 million. The act authorizes the spending of up to $300 million to purchase land. There would also be an additional $7 million in operating expenses.

All of this new spending ignores the fact that the government still owes more than $5 billion to owners of private property that previously has been designated as national parkland. Senator Robert Byrd (D-West Virginia) voiced his opposition to the act by saying: "One does not go out and buy a Cadillac when one cannot make payments on the family Ford." But others were enthused. "This is a tremendous victory that should lift the spirit of conservationists," said Wilderness Society president John Roush.

Representative Billy Tauzin, at the time a Democrat from Lou-
siana (he switched to the Republican party in 1995) had this to say
about the entire Desert Protection Act fiasco: "The way this thing
was fought, it's another example that it's Boston Tea Party time in
terms of the defense of property rights."

If the federal government were demonstrably better at managing wilderness than private property owners, one might be able to
make a case for increasing the government's land holdings. But
clearly the opposite is true. Environmentalists and bureaucrats alike
gain support for national parks by citing tourism and Americans'
love for nature. They then see to it that only a rare few will get to
see it by restricting the construction of lodging facilities or roads in
the parks, banning the use of off-road vehicles and raising park fees.
They cite the need for biodiversity. But they do not maintain biodiversity. They basically say hands off. This often results in one
species becoming dominant in an area (more on this in the next
chapter).

GRAZING

Much of the debate about public lands revolves around grazing. For
a small fee, ranchers are allowed to graze cattle on public lands. But
the current system combines the worst aspects of capitalism, the inherent incompetence of socialism and the worst environmental
practices that can be concocted. "In a culture and economy of free
enterprise, it is the nation's most conspicuous and extensive flirta-
tion with socialism," claim Karl Hess Jr. and Jerry L. Holechek of
the Cato Institute. "Deeply regulated, like other sectors of the economy, it is an industry owned and operated by the U.S. government.
The land and grass are federal property, planning and management
are federal functions, and the workers—the 27,000 ranchers who

own the livestock—are federally licensed, supervised, and subsidized. From the building of fences and watering holes to the setting of details of how, when, and where to graze, grazing on public lands is in every sense a command and control economy."[4]

What has the Interior Department suggested to fix the problem? Higher grazing fees. But, according to Hess and Holechek, "higher grazing fees are unlikely to yield fair market values, stop overgrazing, or end below-cost range use."[5] The General Accounting Office noted that "Because a competitive market does not exist, federal grazing fees must be artificially set in the context of often-conflicting policy objectives."

The solution to this long-standing controversy is to privatize the land as quickly as possible. Much of the Bureau of Land Management land is not environmentally unique or deserving of special protection. If this land were sold at fair market value then free enterprise would be allowed to work, the local government would have a greater tax base and the so-called subsidy would no longer exist.

THE WORST POLLUTER: GOVERNMENT

If the federal government were merely wasting our money when managing public lands, that would be bad enough, but the evidence indicates that it *pollutes* its land far worse than private landowners. "Instead of being a model environmental actor, the government has become part of the problem . . . [It] has generated significant amounts of pollution and caused other stresses on our ecological system." That quote did not come from some rock-ribbed, fire-

---

4. "Beyond the Grazing Fee: An Agenda for Rangeland Reform," Cato Institute Policy Analysis. By Karl Hess Jr. and Jerry L. Holechek, 13 July 1995.
5. Ibid.

breathing conservative, but from the National Performance Review report of Vice President Al Gore.[6]

In 1994, the Department of the Interior released a report conceding that the federal government was the main culprit in the destruction of the nation's wetlands. The Department of Agriculture's farm subsidy program and the Corps of Engineers' damming efforts were mentioned as significantly degrading to the environment. For example, the federal government grants significant subsidies to farmers to grow sugar. This prompts farmers to convert thousands of acres of the Florida Everglades into cropland. For many years the U.S. government paid farmers to drain wetlands in order to increase production of food and fiber.

While greatly restricting private landowners with the provisions of the Endangered Species Act, the government does a poor job with the wilderness it already controls. The Crab Orchard National Wildlife Refuge in Illinois contains 43,500 acres of forest, wetlands, and grasslands, as many as 235,000 migrating Canada geese, at least fifteen species of ducks, forty wintering bald eagles, a huge deer population, wild turkeys, bobcats, and coyotes. Hunting clubs, church camps, and scouting lodges are located within the refuge, which attracts more than 1.3 million visitors each year. It is also a Superfund hazardous waste cleanup site, one of two federal wildlife refuges to receive that dubious distinction. Cleanup will cost at least $56 million and take at least five years, with follow-up testing continuing for thirty years or more. What is worse, the cleanup may be more polluting than the hazardous waste. The government plans to build within the refuge a mobile hazardous materials incinerator. The incinerator would be used to burn about 50,000 cubic yards of soil contaminated with an estimated 70,000 pounds of PCBs and heavy metals. The metals not destroyed in the furnace will be retrieved in the ash, encased in concrete and stored in a dump

---

6. *Washington Post*, 26 April 1994.

on the refuge.[7] The U.S. Government released a report in October 1995 reviewing the status of hazardous waste dumps on federal lands. They counted more than 61,000 dumps on federal lands administered by the Departments of Energy, Defense, Interior and Agriculture, and the National Aeronautics and Space Administration. The report said that complete cleanup could cost $234–$389 billion and take seventy-five years.[8]

The National Forest Service subsidizes timber harvests in many areas that do not produce profitable timber sales. In the Tongass National Forest in Alaska the Forest Service spends $100 per tree harvested and sells each tree for only $2. Only a government could harvest trees at such a tremendous loss. A private landowner would soon go out of business managing his or her land that way. The Forest Service closed logging roads in the Gallatin National Forest in Montana because of concern that grizzly bear habitat was being destroyed. However, because the Forest Service still had a timber goal to meet, it was forced to build new roads to log a new area of the forest. Ironically, this area was also considered prime grizzly bear habitat.[9]

While conducting many of the same activities on its land that private property owners are conducting on theirs, government agencies do not have to go through the same lengthy and costly permit procedures. Bernard N. Goode, a former Corps of Engineers consultant, and attorney Virginia S. Albrecht studied the corps' permitting process and discovered that the largest wetlands exemption went to the U.S. Fish and Wildlife Service to clear over 800 acres of pocosin wetland forest. "Fish and Wildlife's permit," remarked Goode and Albrecht, "which was for 600 acres, an after-the-fact per-

7. *Chicago Tribune*, 30 October 1995.
8. *Daily Environment Report*, 18 October 1995.
9. "Public vs. Private Land Management: Which Is Better for the Environment?" *Property Rights Reader*. By Nicole Arbogast, January 1995.

mit (meaning Fish and Wildlife had done their work before it applied for the permit)—sailed through, requiring only 160 days from public notice to decision, and the Corps did not require any mitigation. In contrast, the second largest permit we reviewed was for the flooding of 319 acres of wetlands for a county water supply project. The county waited over a year after the public notice for its permit and the Corps required 764 acres of mitigation (177 acres of restoration, 525 acres of preservation, and 72 acres of enhancement) and a $175,000 contribution for a nature center and a boardwalk. The smallest application involved 26 square feet of wetland impacts (about half the size of a Ping-Pong table) for residential construction; the application was withdrawn after 450 days."

Robert Best of the Pacific Legal Foundation explained why the government has such a sorry record taking care of its land: "Private ownership naturally gives rise to responsibility and discipline, since the owner's own property is at stake if irrational decisions are made. On the other hand, the more insulated decision makers are from that discipline—as are the bureaucrats managing our public lands—the less likely they are to practice good stewardship. If you doubt this, just look around. Government-managed infrastructure is typically undermaintained. Our national forests are poorly managed compared to privately owned forests. Erosion is more serious on government-owned lands than on those privately owned. Lands managed by the federal Bureau of Land Management are among the most degraded and eroded in the West. Military bases (owned and managed by the government) as one of the biggest sources of pollution in the country."

Warner Glenn, owner of the Malpai ranch in the San Bernardino Valley, expresses a similar sentiment: "Don't get me wrong—there is country around that's hammered. They're darn sure abusing it. But those people don't stay in business too long. Anybody making a living on a ranch would be dumber than a post to ruin the land."

COUNTY SUPREMACY MOVEMENT

Such differences between the way the government and the public take care of their lands have prompted some property rights activists in the West to seek a way to return local control to public lands. Given such names as "the county supremacy movement," "the states' rights movement," and "Sagebrush Rebellion II," these activists have passed resolutions proclaiming sovereignty over public lands within their borders. While many in the mainstream press paint these people as militia-bound wackos, they are mostly just concerned ranchers, farmers, and local politicians trying to alter the top-down relationship the Feds have established. And they have a constitutional basis for their sovereignty claims.

When the thirteen colonies became free sovereign states, all the land within the border of each state was either privately owned or belonged to that state. In 1780, the Continental Congress (then operating under the Articles of Confederation) adopted a resolution requesting the thirteen original states to surrender to the central government their claims to all lands west of their borders to the Mississippi, so that those lands could be sold to private interests in order to pay off the debt incurred by the Revolutionary War. According to the Northwest Ordinance of 1787, these territories would be divided into new states to be admitted into the confederation on the same basis as the original states.

The new Constitution gave Congress the power "to dispose of and make all needful rules and regulations, respecting the Territory belonging to the United States; and nothing in the Constitution shall be construed to prejudice any claim of the United States, or of any particular state." The "equal footing" supporters say that this power refers only to territories, particularly the Northwest Territory, and has no relevance to newly admitted states, which are guaranteed entrance into the Union on an "equal footing" with the original thirteen states. The Framers of the Constitution could have given Congress the authority to own, manage, and control all public lands but they did not. So, the argument goes, those powers are retained by the states, or the people, according to the provisions of the Tenth Amendment.

Catron County in New Mexico was the first of about seventy counties to utilize this complicated but intriguing argument to pass or propose a public lands sovereignty resolution. Nye County in Nevada has been leading the court fight. The county is the size of Vermont and New Hampshire combined, and 93 percent owned by the federal government. The Nye County commissioners felt they were on especially solid ground because the Enabling Act of Nevada contains the following provision: "Enable the people of the territory of Nevada to form a Constitution and State Government and for the admission of such state into the Union on an equal footing with the original states in all respects whatsoever." The "whatsoever" at the end tends to diffuse the federal government's argument that the equal footing doctrine applied only to political rights and not to land.

The U.S. Department of Justice brought suit against Nye County over this issue, making this statement: "Relying upon these faulty claims, the County has bulldozed National Forest lands, opened National Forest roads closed by the Forest Service, damaged natural and archaeological resources, and threatened federal employees with criminal prosecution and other legal action for implementing federal laws." Other government officials clearly believe the residents of Nye County are a bunch of reactionary yahoos. "The actions of county officials could serve to incite further inappropriate behavior," said Kathryn Landreth, U.S. Attorney for the District of Nevada. "Legally, the county supremacy arguments are completely bogus, but politically, they're very potent," said Peter Coppelman, Assistant U.S. Attorney General for environment and natural resources.

Ultimately, U.S. District Judge Lloyd George ruled in favor of the federal government, dealing a sharp blow to the county move-

ment. "The federal government was brought to the point of recognizing that the wishes of the people who live with their decisions on
a day-to-day basis can't be ignored," said Roger Marzulla, Nye
County's attorney. There are no plans to appeal.[10]

The idea that the people who use public lands are inconsequential permeates the attitudes of government bureaucrats. It is not
surprising, therefore, to find in some of these same government
agencies the belief that people in general are inconsequential. Indeed,
some of the "defenders of the wilderness" would prefer to keep people as far away from it as possible.

---

10. "Nye County Loses Land Dispute Battle With Feds," Associated Press, 15 March 1996.

6

UNDISTURBED BY MAN

"Yes, we have taken away some of the rights of the people living in the Adirondacks, but that's the penalty they have to pay for living there."[1]

——FORMER NEW YORK GOVERNOR MARIO CUOMO

The lack of respect for property rights exhibited by many environmentalists may be baffling to you. I know it was to me, at first. Don't these people own property, too? Don't activists—particularly liberal activists—have a healthy skepticism and distrust of the police powers of the state? Don't the same people who pride themselves on their support of the civil rights movement see the plight of individuals beset by unfair laws? Only after years of dealing with government officials and professional environmental activists did I come to realize that they see the dirt, trees, and animals as their *con-*

---

1. "Greens vs. Property Rights: The Environmental Backlash," by Jonathan H. Adler *Property Rights Reader,* January 1995.

stituency. As they see it, the planet is under assault and it cannot defend itself. It cannot even speak for itself. Only *they* stand between the vanishing wilderness and its mortal enemy . . . man. There is no sense of a balance between man and nature. Nature is in harmony by itself, and man's interference upsets that balance. Thus, man's activities are *unnatural* and must be curbed. Since, in their view, humans are motivated by self-interest above all, they cannot be trusted to care for the planet—they must be coerced. Better yet, they must be physically removed from "wilderness areas" to avoid the inevitable contamination caused by their presence. Federal wilderness areas in the United States are defined, by law, to be places "where the earth and community of life are untrammeled by man, where man himself is a visitor who does not remain." Taken to its logical extremes (and a growing number of groups are doing so), such a dogma calls for a reduction in human population.

Once you accept the delineation of plants, dirt, and animals as innocent victims worthy of protection, it is possible to depict the human beings whose actions cause this perceived victimization as villains or criminals. Some environmental zealots have vivid ways of expressing their positions on the effects of humans on nature. William Perry Pendley, in his powerful book *War on the West,* catalogued some of the worst:

- "Loggers losing their jobs because of spotted owl legislation is, in my eyes, no different than people being out of work after the furnaces of Dachau shut down."—David Brower, former executive director of the Sierra Club.
- "Mankind is the most dangerous, destructive, selfish and unethical animal on earth."—Michael W. Fox, vice president of the Humane Society of the United States.
- "Mankind is the biggest blight on the face of the earth. Six million people died in concentration camps, but six billion broiler

97

chickens will die this year in slaughterhouses."—Ingrid Newkirk, national director of People for the Ethical Treatment of Animals.

- "Human happiness and certainly human fecundity are not as important as a wild and healthy planet. I know social scientists who remind me that people are part of nature, but it isn't true. Somewhere along the line—at about a billion years ago and maybe half of that—we quit the contract and became a cancer. We have become a plague upon ourselves and upon the Earth . . . some of us can only hope for the right virus to come along."—David M. Graber, a research biologist with the National Park Service.

- "[T]he greatest environmental disaster coming out of the Yellowstone Park fire was its failure to burn up [the town of] West Yellowstone. In the fierce competition between Wyoming and Montana for the ugliest town, West Yellowstone is the easy winner. What a wonderful thing it would have been to reduce all that neon clutter and claptrap to ashes."—Scott Reed, National Audubon Society board member.

Whether this type of rhetoric is representative of the views of the average environmentalist is certainly open to debate. What cannot be denied are the ostensible efforts to remove the human element from nature. Martin Littion, a board member of the Sierra Club, said, "The only way we can save any wilderness in this country is to make it harder to get into, and harder to stay in once you get there." This fundamental principle has already been put into effect by a coalition of environmentalists and federal officials and has been translated into even more radical proposals for land use across the United States.

Undisturbed by Man

THE WILDLANDS PROJECT

The organization Earth First! has received media attention connected to the spiking of trees. The spikes, when contacted by lumber saws, can cause serious bodily harm to timber workers. But Earth First! also has its propositions for land use in the United States. The group and its founder, Dave Foreman, are credited with developing the Wildlands Project. The concept behind it is clearly spelled out: "[W]e see wilderness as the home for unfettered life, free from industrial human intervention. [Wilderness means:] "Vast landscapes without roads, dams, motorized vehicles, powerlines, overflights, or other artifacts of civilization, where evolutionary and ecological processes that represent four billion years of Earth wisdom can continue."[2]

The Wildlands Project would set up millions of acres of wilderness preserves. Inside these areas all evidence of civilizations would be eradicated. There would be no houses, no roads, no power lines—no man-made structures of any kind. By any means necessary, the wildlands would be restored to the condition the planners believe North America was in before the arrival of the first humans. Oregon biologist Reed Noss thinks these wilderness preserves would have to contain "at least half of the land area of the coterminous states." But even that is not enough. These zones would be surrounded by "buffer areas" in which human activity would be severely curtailed. Eventually, people would exist only on reservations surrounded by the natural wilderness.

Far-fetched? Perhaps, but writer Russell Madden cites ongoing projects designed to make the Wildlands Project dream a reality: "Efforts are currently underway to set aside 139,000 square miles in

2. *Wild Earth,* (Special Issue), "The Wildlands Project," 1992, Cenozoic Society, Inc., Canton, NY, inside cover.

the Great Plains for a buffalo sanctuary; the Paseo Pantera project seeks to connect wilderness areas in Central America; British Columbia is linking a new 4,000 square mile park with Alaska and the Yukon Territory to create a 33,000 square mile preserve; Congress is considering setting aside 11,000 square miles in California; the Nevada Biodiversity Project seeks to set aside hundreds of square miles of mountains; and Noss recently received $150,000 from the Pew Charitable Funds to further planning for wildlands set-asides."[3]

California already has 4.4 million acres in fifty-three designated wilderness areas. The California Desert Protection Act restricts road use and off-road vehicles in the newest preserves. Large parts of this vast territory are restricted to hikers and horseback riders, meaning that most Americans will never see these areas except by airplane. This did not seem to disturb Senator Barbara Boxer (D-California): "As we look to the future years when we are no longer here, it seems to me that it is our very grave responsibility to leave environments behind that are untouched." Recent reports show that a large number of wilderness areas get fewer visitors each year. The 500,000-acre Trinity Alps Wilderness in northern California is the state's second-largest wilderness area. Yet its remoteness means it gets fewer visitors than wilderness areas around Lake Tahoe or nearer Loss Angeles. The 13,787-acre Santa Rosa Wilderness, south of Palm Springs, California, estimated only 200 daily visitors in 1994. Apparently, wildlands enthusiasts are already getting their wish.

HUMANS VS. ANIMALS

This hands-off approach has already led to harmful consequences for both humans and wildlife. The U.S. Department of Agriculture has

---

3. "Eco-Fascism," by Russell Madden, *The Freeman,* April 1995.

logged a steady increase in complaints about wild animals in the past ten years. In 1994, it tracked, relocated or killed 42 million problem animals, 6 million more than the previous year. Each year, the animals cause half a billion dollars in damage and kill half a million livestock. Mountain lions have fatally attacked two women in California in the past year, the first in the state since 1900.

"There are probably more wild creatures in the cities than the same amount of forest land would support," said Paul Wertz of the California Department of Fish and Game. These animals do not seem to mind the presence of humans at all. "A raccoon in the forest might have to forage over miles to get enough to eat," said Dairen Simpson, Santa Clara County wildlife specialist. "In the city, he just rolls his fat body out from under the deck by the pool, wolfs down three or four pounds of pet food and goes back to bed." San Jose Municipal Court Judge Robert Ambrose described the scene around his house: "Last night, there were 14 deer and numerous raccoons and possums here, 50 feet from city streets. I put motion lights up, and they're going on and off all night long. The animals own the place."

When "animals own the place," what transpires is not harmonious by any stretch of the imagination. What tends to happen is assimilation by one side or the other—that is, either the animals are forced to live on human terms, or humans are forced to deal with animals in animal terms. When the former occurs, you get many tragic stories of animals unable to fend for themselves. When the latter occurs, you put more and more human beings in "kill or be killed" confrontations with dangerous wildlife. Both situations are best illustrated by recent incidents with bears.

A Colorado official called 1995 "the summer of the bears from hell." The *New York Times* described this close encounter in Conifer, Colorado: "On a rainy night, Jeannie Flavin and her three small children cowered in their remote hilltop house here as two black bear cubs outside banged repeatedly on the sliding glass door leading to the living room. Near the cubs, the 250-pound mother bear was prowling. A neighbor of the Flavins crept up behind the bears. Suddenly, the mother bear wheeled around and charged at him. The neighbor raised his Winchester rifle and fired. When the shooting stopped, the bear and her two cubs were dead, the Flavins were saved and their $150,000 alpaca herd was unscathed."

A dangerous situation ended happily, right? Wrong. Karl Mayne, the neighbor who saved the Flavins' lives (and his own) with his rifle has received so many death threats that he has changed his telephone number. What's worse, Mayne was charged in Jefferson County Court with cruelty, killing wildlife, and hunting illegally.

Black bears are by no measure an endangered species in Colorado. The total bear population in the state is over 10,000. The bears are omnivores and an adult bear will routinely eat for twenty hours and up to fifty pounds of food per day. The burgeoning bear population has led to increased attacks on livestock. The number of sheep and lambs killed by bears hit 450 in 1994, when Colorado topped the nation in sheep killed by bears. The bears are becoming bolder in approaching human habitation. At a Boy Scout camp, a bear had "ripped door off freezer locked with hasp" and another bear "tore car apart looking for remains of toasted cheese sandwich."

The environmentalists and the government took their usual stance—against the humans. "Everyone wants their piece of the wild Rockies, and then they set about killing what makes it inconvenient," said Darrell Knuffke, regional director of the Wilderness Society. "Problem bears are the result of 'problem' people," read the script of an information slide show developed by state wildlife officials.

On the opposite end of the spectrum are the dump bears of Willits, California. For years, these California black bears have been leaving the surrounding mountains to feast at the Willits dump, six miles east of town. The bear population grew by leaps and bounds. In fact, the landfill has become such an attraction for bears that their population is about five times what the natural environment would support. Many of the bears are fourth or fifth generation garbage addicts. And no wonder. The Willits dump includes leftovers from the county's finest restaurants.

The landfill is supposed to be covered over and closed next year, leaving residents worried about where the bears will next go for food. "Moving bears is expensive and doesn't work, either," said state wildlife biologist Alan Buckmann. "We kept taking one over 50 miles away, and he always beat us back to the dump. They put up a fence and the bears climbed over it."

"It's basically impossible to take a bear trained to be a garbage bear and take him some place in hopes he'll unlearn it or forget about it," said Doug Updike, senior biologist with the state Department of Fish and Game. "There's no place to move another bear—we're brimming with bears." Ken Dials of the county Humane Society had a different view. "We're not going to let anything happen to those bears—no matter what," he said.[4]

Human activity certainly has an effect—sometimes an injurious effect—on the environment. But the coalition of bureaucrats and activists have already gone well beyond the realm of reason in restricting human activity. A San Diego school district prohibited car washes as fund-raisers for school programs because car wash water entered into the storm sewer system, and so could be in violation of the Clean Water Act.[5]

Environmentalists picketed the annual convention of the Casket and Funeral Supply Association because, they claim, the manufacturing of mahogany coffins is depleting the rain forests of South America. They say people should choose a coffin made of metal, pine or, better yet, fiberboard made from recycled telephone books. The fact is that only 1 percent of deceased Americans, about 8,000 peo-

---

4. "Bear Trap: Garbage Addicts May Face Death Sentence," by Michael Dorgan, *San Jose Mercury News,* 17 August 1995.
5. *The Wall Street Journal,* 18 October 1995.

ple per year—are buried in mahogany coffins. This amount of mahogany is inconsequential and the expense keeps more people from using it. Meanwhile, the Environmental Protection Agency's regional administrator spent $20,000 of taxpayer funds putting a mesquite wood floor in his Chicago office suite. No protesters could be found.[6]

It does not stop there. The Park Service is requiring people in the Mojave National Park to build campfires in "fire pans" or garbage lids to protect the *ground*. A fourteen-year-old Illinois Boy Scout was separated from his troop in the Pecos Wilderness in New Mexico. For more than twenty-four hours, the Forest Service refused to permit a helicopter to land to bring him to safety. "We made a call according to our Wilderness Act," said a Forest Service spokesperson. "I guess some people can perceive it as a bad call."

UNINTENDED CONSEQUENCES

One of the core beliefs of the eco-federal coalition is that there are no such things as unintended consequences. There used to be grizzly bears in California, they say, so let's get some grizzly bears and put them back in California. There were more forests before Columbus arrived, so we will stop cutting down trees and restore that acreage to woodland. The hypocrisy is that in the name of removing human impact on nature, government is required to intervene mightily. The U.S. government is spending $2.2 million to reintroduce the endangered black-footed ferret into a valley north of Medicine Bow, Wyoming. Since 1991, 228 captive-born ferrets have been turned loose. Only seven animals are known to have survived. Do the math.

6. "IG: Too Much Glitter in Federal Buildings," *Federal Times*, 23 October 1995.

The environmental attack on the timber industry has had more than its share of unintended consequences. Lumber prices have hit all-time highs and twenty-three lumber mills closed in 1993. The price of lumber is extremely volatile. What effect has this had on the housing business? In 1994, about 13,000 houses nationwide were framed in steel; this year there will be close to 40,000. As familiarity grows, one in four houses may be framed in steel by next year. Building more house frames out of steel instead of wood has environmental consequences as well, perhaps enough to counteract the restriction on timber. According to a report prepared by the Committee on Renewable Resources for Industrial Materials, it takes more than seventeen times the energy to produce a ton of steel studs than a ton of softwood lumber.

Markets are able to adjust to restricted supplies by cutting production or finding alternative materials. Small towns rarely have the same capability. This chain of events has been repeated in many places across the country. The saw mill shuts down so logging profits and fees disappear. Most of the land remains under Forest Service jurisdiction so it cannot be taxed. Since there are no jobs, families leave the area. Property values drop. Tax revenues drop. The community dies. Happy Camp, California, was listed by the National Association of Counties as one of the ten most endangered communities in America. In the mid-1980s, the town had four saw mills and double its present population of 1,200. In order to protect the spotted owl and the marbled murrelet, the Forest Service cut the timber quota in the area from 50 million board feet to 8 million board feet. The last mill shut down last year. "The tree huggers killed the town," said property agent Charlie Bowling. Now 65 percent of the Happy Camp population receive public assistance. People who were self-supporting and confident are now defeated and on welfare. Is that the direction we want to take?

The believers in Big Government say that's why we need government funding for job retraining. The Clinton administration spent $5 million trying to retrain northwest loggers into new careers—like documenting plant species in the now-protected forest. There's a growth industry for you. The California Department of Conservation produces a publication called "Good, Green Jobs." It is illuminating to see what government considers a model corporation. One company mentioned is U.S. Electricar. U.S. Electricar created five joint ventures and bought out four competing electric vehicle firms. In March 1995, the company announced two plant closures, laid off sixty employees and reported a loss of $16.5 million on sales of $3.7 million.

THE MYTH OF "UNTOUCHED" WILDERNESS

Instead of buying into the rhetoric of "land rape" and "environmental holocaust," let's see exactly what humans do to the land. Let's examine both its effect on the earth and on your life.

In his book *Uncommon Ground: Toward Reinventing Nature,* William Cronon tells the truth about wilderness: "Ever since the 19th century, celebrating wilderness has been an activity mainly for well-to-do city folks. Country people generally know far too much about working the land to regard unworked land as their ideal . . . The movement to set aside national parks and wilderness areas followed hard on the heels of the final Indian wars, in which the prior human inhabitants of these regions were rounded up and moved onto reservations so that tourists could safely enjoy the illusion that they were seeing their nation in its pristine, original state—in the new morning of God's own creation. Meanwhile, its original inhabitants were kept out by dint of force, their earlier uses of the land redefined as inappropriate or even illegal."

Cronon rips the veil from the cognitive dissonance employed by many environmentalists: "The dream of an unworked landscape is very much the fantasy of people who have never themselves had to work the land to make a living—urban folk for whom food comes from a supermarket or a restaurant instead of a field, and for whom the wooden houses in which they live and work apparently have no meaningful connection to the forests in which trees grow and die. Only people whose relation to the land was already alienated could hold up wilderness as a model for human life in nature, for the romantic ideology of wilderness leaves no place in which human beings can actually make their living from the land."

Writer Stephen Budiansky got even more specific about the unfounded belief that wilderness areas should be "untouched": "The grasses in my field are aliens, timothy and bluegrass and red clover brought to America by seventeenth-century English settlers trying for a better hay crop. The sheep and horses and cattle are alien imports too. But for their constant grazing, and for the annual visit of the haying machines, the open acres that stretch from my window to the copse at the bottom of the hill would in just a few years' time be choked with brambles and red cedars. But even that could hardly be counted a natural process; the return of woods to abandoned farm fields is not nature reclaiming her birthright but nature led only farther astray. Red cedars readily take over abandoned pastures today only because centuries of grazing by livestock has unnaturally suppressed the hardwoods, such as oaks, that would otherwise outcompete the red cedars; the very abundance of red cedar today is an artifact of the dietary preferences of imported farm animals."[7]

The stated policy for national parks in America is for a preservation of an area as it supposedly was before the arrival of Columbus in 1492. This policy does not address the practice by Native Americans of burning vegetation to promote new growth and attract game. The policy does not address the fact that there are five times the number of deer in Virginia now than there were before the

---

7. "Unpristine Nature," by Stephen Budiansky, *The American Enterprise*, September/October 1995.

Europeans arrived. Deer reduce the number of songbirds, woodland wildflowers, and overall biodiversity. Elk destroy aspen and willows. Insects and disease destroy about 4.5 billion cubic feet of timber each year.

Should wild horses be hunted down and destroyed? Europeans brought them to this continent. Thousands of plant species were imported to America. Should they be uprooted? "Time and again," writes Budiansky, "nature lovers launch earnest efforts to 'save' from human depredation landscapes or wildlife populations that are nothing but the recent and unnatural creations of man's presence, while they rail against the very kinds of 'interference' that have for millennia shaped and perpetuated the nature they love. To literally let nature 'take her course' is not one of the options any longer. The irony is that to have nature be 'natural' requires constant human intrusion. Restoration projects have been remarkably successful in reconstructing and maintaining native savannas and prairies through the use of clear-cutting followed by regular, deliberate burning. The artificial turns out to be more 'natural' than the natural. No matter what we choose to do, nature is being shaped by man. We can recognize the fact and try to deal with it, or we can ignore it and accept the consequences. The one thing we cannot do is remove human influence simply by closing our eyes to it."[8]

CAN WE LIVE WITHOUT MINING?

Apart from its effect on the "natural" environment, are we willing to give up what human activity—particularly human industrial and agricultural activity—does for our health and way of life. The mining industry is often painted as vicious earth molesters. On the con-

---

8. Ibid.

trary, today's miner's are very land-efficient, utilizing only 508,000—a mere .022 percent of the nation's land area—to extract all the minerals we need. This is less land than we use for airports. I will wager that few environmentalists are aware of their own reliance on the mining industry. The Arizona Mining Association provides these statistics:

- The average U.S. citizen will consume 40,000 pounds of nonfuel minerals annually during his or her lifetime.
- At this rate of consumption, the U.S. Bureau of Mines estimates that a baby born in 1991 will consume during his or her lifetime the following minerals:
    —Sand and gravel for homes, schools, offices, factories, and roads: 1,238,100 pounds.
    —Iron for house appliances, kitchen utensils, cars, ships, and buildings: 32,700 pounds.
    —Salt for plastic products, detergents, water softeners, and foods: 28,200 pounds.
    —Clay for bricks, paper, paint, glass, and pottery: 26,600 pounds.
    —Aluminum for beverage cans, house siding, and aluminum foil and as an alloy for pipes, steam irons, cookware, and aircraft: 3,600 pounds.
    —Copper for electric motors, generators, communications equipment, and electrical wiring: 1,500 pounds.
    —Lead for car batteries, electric components, and solder: 800 pounds.
    —Zinc for protective coatings on steel and chemical compounds for rubber and paint and as an alloy to make brass: 750 pounds.

Food Doesn't Come From the Supermarket

Agriculture has by far had the greatest effect on the environment. But the benefits of farming are simply too numerous to ignore. Tree farmers and orchardists plant nearly 3 billion trees on their property each year. Farmers and ranchers not in the tree-producing business plant an additional 9 million trees. The Agriculture Council of American provides these statistics:

- Each year one American farmer provides food and fiber for 129 people—97 in the United States and 32 abroad.
- By 2000, agriculture is expected to generate 25 percent of the U.S. Gross Domestic Product.
- One-fourth of the world's beef and nearly one-fifth of the world's grain, milk, and eggs are produced in the United States.
- Glycerine, a by-product derived from vegetable oils and animal fats, has more than 1,500 commercial applications from cosmetics to drugs.
- With modern methods, one acre of land in the United States can produce:
  —42,000 pounds of strawberries or
  —24,000 pounds of navel oranges or
  —11,000 heads of lettuce or
  —25,400 pounds of potatoes or
  —8,900 pounds of sweet corn or
  —640 pounds of cotton lint.

Recently, environmentalists have begun to join forces with the population control movement to promote a concept called "sustainable development." The organization Zero Population Growth rents space in the National Wildlife Federation's $40-million office building in Washington, D.C. Their premise is that the world (particularly the United States) is consuming natural resources at such a rate that they will soon be depleted. This is utter nonsense, as proved by the falling prices of every known raw material in this century. Sustainable development advocates also fail to account for economic adjustment. In the nineteenth century, a shortage of horses would have been catastrophic to the nation's economy. Today, of course, we have fuel-powered vehicles—which, I should add, are much less polluting than an equivalent number of horses.

Are we running out of food? No. Enough food could be raised to provide an American-type diet for 35.1 billion people, more than seven times the present world population. Enough food could be produced for over 100 billion people if they were fed a Japanese-level diet. Are we running out of space? No. Only three-tenths of 1 percent of the earth's land surface is used for human settlements. Are we running out of arable land? No. We use less than one-ninth of the earth's ice-free land area to raise all agricultural products.[9]

"On average," writes economist Julian Simon, "people throughout the world have been living longer and eating better than ever before. The real prices of food and of every other raw material are lower now than in earlier decades and centuries, indicating a trend of increased natural resource availability rather than increased scarcity. The major air and water pollutions in the advanced countries have been lessening rather than worsening. In short, every single measure of material and environmental welfare in the United States has improved rather than deteriorated."

WHAT IS NATURAL?

Removing man from the balance of nature is fundamentally flawed. Nature left alone is not nature in harmony. Some species tend to

---

9. Jacqueline Kasun, *The War Against Population,* Ignatius Press, 1988, p. 38.

dominate others, reducing biodiversity instead of promoting it. My lawn might be more "natural" if I let it grow unhindered. But lawns left unmowed and untended become unsightly fire hazards, homes for weeds and pests. My dog might be more "natural" if I let him run loose. But dogs roaming free through the neighborhood do not live in harmony with the rest of God's creatures, but form packs, killing and eating smaller animals and polluting the water. Dog productivity appears to be constant over time, so overpopulation is always a danger, both to the dogs and other animals. Does it make any difference it we talk about forests instead of lawns, bears instead of dogs?

Then if untrammeled nature is not really "natural," for what purpose are our civil rights being trammeled? Property rights in America are being sacrificed for a vision that we cannot see. It is not the vision of the average American, but that of an urban, upper-class elite who are completely convinced that their plan for your property is better than your plan. Their goal is control of what is yours. And if endangered species, wetlands, and anti-pollution regulations will not get it for them, then they will find other means.

7

THE SLIPPERY SLOPE

"When there is doubt concerning the magnitude of [development] impacts, the public interest in averting them must outweigh the private interest of the commercial entrepreneur."

—U.S. SUPREME COURT JUSTICE JOHN PAUL STEVENS

The government can literally seize control of your life when it finds endangered species or wetlands on your property. But that's not the only way it works. Government officials are bold and innovative when it comes to figuring out ways to take what rightfully belongs to you. Bureaucrats feel they are "promoting the general welfare" when they secure easements, bicycle and hiking trails, historic areas, archaeological digs, and property that maintains scenic views, ambiance, or environmentally correct lifestyles. What all these rationalizations have in common is that they violate the Fifth Amendment. While the property owner is still required to pay taxes on his land or home, the government has taken it for public use without providing just compensation. My personal experience with local and state government over property usage may be illustrative.

A railroad right-of-way passed through my family ranch in California. The right-of-way had not been used for many years. The tracks were washed out in many places and eventually were all removed, leaving only the rail bed. When the right-of-way was established in the late 1800s, it was for "railroad purposes only" and would revert back to the adjoining property owners if the railroad ever abandoned it. In the 1980s it was abandoned and that is when the controversy started.

A local park district had long sought the establishment of recreational trails throughout the rolling hills of the area. Officials were not deterred by the fact that the land in question was almost all private property. The park district had already been successful in placing several trails on the map. The next step was moving to protect the "viewshed" (everything that you can see) of these trails. The district sought to halt all construction of homes and other structures within the viewshed—without any compensation whatsoever. The park district sought this abandoned railroad right-of-way as a recreational trail through the property of two dozen local ranchers and that of my family. The local park district was unwilling to erect fencing, pick up trash that accumulated, or patrol the trails for the public's (and our) safety. This, combined with the potential harm being done to grazing livestock, presented us with many new costs and liabilities. We were very concerned that it would interfere with our ability to conduct business on our own property.

If the public, represented by an agency such as a park district, determines that it is in the public interest to take a significant part of the value of someone's private land, then the public should pay. The private landowner should not be expected to bear the entire cost of what is supposed to be a public good. My neighbors and I challenged this law because we believed it was a property right being taken from us without compensation. Several years and several hundred thousand dollars later, we fought to a mixed conclusion. Lawsuits such as ours convinced the environmental groups to induce

Congress to pass the "Rails to Trails Act," which dictates that abandoned right-of-ways become part of a trail system, completely bypassing the private property rights of adjoining landowners and unilaterally breaking a contract that was made in good faith many years ago.

DOLAN V. TIGARD

A similar such case reached the United States Supreme Court. *Dolan v. Tigard* was noteworthy because it was one of the few cases where the Supreme Court placed a distinct limit on government overreach. Florence Dolan wanted to replace her plumbing supply store with a larger one. The city of Tigard, Oregon, was willing to grant her a permit only if she would deed to the city 10 percent of her 1.67-acre property for pedestrian and bicycle pathways, a municipal park, and then reconstruct a storm drainage channel. Dolan believed this to be a form of government extortion, and took the city to court. Despite the fact that the Solicitor General argued on behalf of Tigard, Dolan won her case in a 5-4 Supreme Court decision.

Chief Justice William Rehnquist delivered the court's opinion: "The government may not require a person to give up a constitutional right—here the right to receive just compensation when property is taken for public use—in exchange for a discretionary benefit conferred by the government where the property sought has little or no relationship to the benefit. . . . We see no reason why the Takings Clause of the Fifth Amendment, as much a part of the Bill of Rights as the First Amendment or Fourth Amendment, should be relegated to the status of a poor relation. . . . A strong public desire to improve the public condition [will not] warrant achieving the desire by a shorter cut than the constitutional way of paying for the change."

HISTORIC PRESERVATION

One of the many groups that filed "friends of the court" briefs in support of the city of Tigard was the National Trust for Historic Preservation. A private, nonprofit organization, the trust receives an annual $7 million grant from National Park Service. The trust's mission is to preserve structures and areas of cultural and historic importance. But "preserve" takes on a whole new meaning when the trust applies it. In 1993, the trust placed the entire state of Vermont on its annual list of the eleven most endangered places in America. The following year it added Cape Cod. The organization's penchant for empire-building is clear from the identity of some of the "historic areas" it has decided to protect. These include a vintage McDonald's restaurant in Downey, California, and Detroit's Tiger Stadium.

The trust has had a running battle with Wal-Mart, the huge discount store chain. The trust wants Wal-Mart to locate in "smaller, more sensitively designed stores in downtowns . . ." The fact that the majority of Wal-Mart's customers go there because it is large and conveniently located is of no concern to the trust. The National Trust for Historic Preservation wants more than to just preserve the Gettysburg battlefield or Thomas Jefferson's estate at Monticello. At a 1994 conference the group advanced a new paradigm of 1) restoring historic buildings, neighborhoods, and human lives; 2) reweaving the built environment; 3) rebuilding authentic community; 4) reconstructing the local economy; and 5) renewing human connections.

Property owners across America know what's coming when a government-funded organization plans on "renewing the built environment." Advancing the metaphor, it means "tearing the fabric" of private property and "tailoring" it to suit the whims of the appointed few. The trust is not the only organization restricting property rights in the name of historic preservation. There are over two thousand state and local historic preservation ordinances throughout the

116

United States. The effect on homeowners is far-reaching and severe. Joel Gambord found himself in big trouble because he remodeled part of the famous John Steinbeck house in Monte Sereno, California. Steinbeck wrote *The Grapes of Wrath* in the house, but it had many owners between the time Steinbeck worked there and Gambord bought it. Gambord found termites and dry rot in the timbers. He removed the guest wing's exterior siding, overhang, and part of its porch before the condition spread. Upon discovering the "misdeed," the city immediately slapped a "stop work" order on Gambord and threatened legal action. Gambord couldn't understand the fuss. The home had been remodeled several times. What the city wanted to preserve might not have even been present when Steinbeck worked there.

Most Americans would find it an invasion of their rights to have to consult a group of political appointees before they hang shutters on their house. But if your home is designated a "landmark," there is no limit to the restrictions that government can apply to it. Writer James Bovard has spent many years chronicling government abuses. In his book *Shakedown,* he lists some of the intrusions visited by historic preservation ordinances:

"The New York Landmarks Commission imposed preservation controls over the 1958 *interior* of the Four Seasons restaurant. Preservation bureaucrats prohibited the owner from removing two hanging sculptures, changing the long draperies, or modifying the restaurant's bar. The New York Landmarks Commission also banned residents of SoHo in Manhattan from planting any trees in their neighborhood. Why? Because the commission wanted to preserve the grimy industrial feel of the neighborhood that existed in the late 1800s. The same commission prohibits residents in many New York apartment buildings from replacing their old windows (even when they are broken) with newer, better-insulating windows. Instead, the residents must spend three or four times more to install old-fashioned windows that satisfy the Landmarks Commission staff. . . . Dennis Foley, a resident [of Arlington County, Virginia], ignited a major fight in 1993 when he sought permission to install wood-grain vinyl shutters on his windows. The review board insisted that he use wood shutters instead—even though they cost twice as much and require much more maintenance. Though the difference between the wood-grain and real wood shutters would not be visible to people passing in the street near Foley's house, the review board refused to budge."[1]

Rich or poor, liberal or conservative, property owners find themselves under siege. In March 1995, the Kennedy family filed a lawsuit attempting to block the Palm Beach Landmarks Preservation Committee from designating its vacation estate in that city as a historic site. Kennedy lawyers claimed that building restrictions imposed as a result of the designation would lower the family's $7 million asking price for the estate, which was up for sale at the time.

The cult of preservation extends into the area of archaeology as well. If your home sits on top of ancient burial grounds, watch out! Jay Colvin of Eden, Arizona, fresh from his run-in with the Army Corps of Engineers (see chapter four) tells of restrictions on his own property in the name of preservation: "We have been hit from other agencies that are involved with Indian ruins in our area. We have a very old Hohokam village on our private property. We contacted the University of Arizona when we were told what we had. This was years before the laws pertaining to Indian artifacts came into play. We protected the area while the University dug up the artifacts. We

---

1. James Bovard, *Shakedown: How the Government Screws You from A to Z,* Viking Press, 1995, pp. 53–54.

did not profit from it in any way. We could have; we could have destroyed a part of history. What we got for our troubles was a total ban from using our own property. We could not even drive on the road going to our property. Not only did they deny us access to our own road, they indicated that we were liable for anyone else that may use the road and disturb any bones. We are also liable for anyone who decides to go dig with or without our permission. Since the Hohokam buried the ashes and bones in the floor of their homes, it is impossible to do anything with this property. We still pay taxes on it. We cannot sell it, there is no value because of the ruins."

There is no limit to what can be designated for preservation. The National Trust for Historic Preservation was very upset about construction in the area around Thomas Jefferson's estate in Monticello. The organization wanted to have legislation passed at the local level to prohibit building in any area that could be *seen* from Monticello. As one clever commentator put it, the trust violated Jefferson's views in order to preserve Jefferson's view.

It may seem comical that people's constitutional rights could be violated in order to guarantee someone else's unobstructed view of the mountains, the prairies, or the oceans white with foam. It may seem criminal that those same rights could be violated to preserve the "ambiance" of a selected geographic area. But such violations occur every day. Developer Paul Gould wanted to build a resort and health spa complex on property he purchased in 1983 in southern San Mateo County, California. The Sierra Club and the Committee for Green Foothills sued to block construction. "I don't have anything against fitness centers, but why would you waste a magnificent coastal setting and put something there that doesn't relate to the area in any way?" said Lennie Roberts, legislative advocate for the Committee for Green Foothills. "You can put fitness centers anywhere, but there's only one coast of California and what we put there should really relate to the coast."

The California Coastal Commission will not allow farmers to

construct greenhouses on their coastal fields. Planners in San Mateo County said that the structures clash with "surrounding natural landscape features," and "the visual impact is often considered obtrusive."

In Fairbanks, Alaska, a homeowner was granted a zoning variance to build a five-story house. His neighbor across the road lives in a different section of the subdivision and therefore was not consulted. He sued because now he cannot see Birch Hill. He can still see two rivers, the Alaska Range, and most of Fairbanks, but without Birch Hill he was distraught. The neighbor sued to have the house torn down. Judge James Beistline ruled that the owner had to tear down the top floor of his building and change the pitch of his roof so that the plaintiff can see over the house. The homeowner appealed the decision, claiming the changes will require him to spend an additional $200,000 and will reduce his home's value by 50 percent.

Not too many taxpayers are aware of the existence of a federal Grand Canyon Visibility Commission. As with most federal agencies, the commission wants to extend the scope of its powers. It recently claimed its jurisdiction extended to the "Colorado Plateau," which would encompass millions of acres of Arizona, Colorado, and New Mexico. The Commission believes it can improve the view of the Grand Canyon by reducing emissions from cars, trucks, and lawn mowers *in Los Angeles.*

In San Francisco, the Planning Commission suddenly decided that a flower stand on Post Street was a "nuisance." An injunction was filed against Harold Hoogasian, the flower stand owner, by Sidney Unobskey, the commission's president. Unobskey claims the flower stand is "too big" and "in the way." The stand has been at the same location for over forty years.

Some localities require lawn sprinklers for new homes. Others require a permit for painting . . . *interiors.* Still others prohibit your house from looking like other houses on the same street. Under stringent zoning laws, just about anything can be regulated. "We address every possible condition a person living their life could encounter," said Ellen Uguccioni, historic preservation administrator for Coral Gables, Florida. "Every single item that could possibly cause a visual nuisance or any other nuisance we attempt to regulate through our zoning code."

TWILIGHT ZONING

Most localities in the United States have zoning laws. There are restrictions on the types of buildings that may be constructed in populated areas. Towns may zone some areas for residences, others for small businesses, and others for industrial use. There may be limits on signs, noise, or emissions. Most property owners are content to abide by zoning laws. Where they feel their rights are being violated is when government makes it impossible for them to put the property to the use for which it has been zoned. Government officials are also masters of using zoning laws to obtain concessions from property owners. When they do this, they often turn the Fifth Amendment on its head.

The problem arises because government officials often believe that when they zone an area for a particular purpose, they have acquired for the public a *right to* that particular use. By this reasoning, when a property owner seeks a zoning change he or she must first compensate the public (read: government) for its loss of that usage. It is a hypocritical, but fiendishly clever way to shake down property owners for land or fees the government wants. A good example of this process is seen in the case of *Ehrlich v. City of Culver City*.

Ehrlich operated a private tennis club on a 2.4-acre site in Culver City, California, but was unable to turn a profit. At the time, the land was zoned commercial with a specific plan providing for a sports facility. In 1988, he closed the facility, donated a large amount of equipment to the city, and proposed a $10 million townhouse condominium project for the site.

Culver City officials denied the request on the grounds that the zoning change would mean a loss of recreational facilities. Their reasoning was curious, because Ehrlich ran a private club and besides, the club was already out of business. Ehrlich sued. The city then agreed to approve the project on the condition that Ehrlich pay $280,000—the estimated cost of building four new tennis courts—in compensation for the city's "loss." As an added bonus, the city demanded that Ehrlich place public art on his property, or pay an additional fee of $33,220. City officials claimed that "the opportunity for creation of cultural and artistic resources is diminished" by development. The case shows that the city has decreed that Ehrlich will own a tennis club, whether he wants to or not. His only release from his servitude is to buy his freedom—to the tune of over $300,000.[2]

TOM AND DORIS DODD

In the typical topsy-turvy way that governments work, we have instances of one branch of government fighting tooth and nail to prevent logging from taking place, while another branch uses zoning laws to force people to log against their will. In 1983, Tom and Doris Dodd decided to buy forty acres in Hood River, Oregon, for their retirement home. In 1985, they began the planning process. To their dismay, the zoning law affecting their parcel was changed after they had purchased the property and returned home to Houston, Texas. Under the new rules, the Dodds could use their land only to grow and harvest timber. The only way they could build a home was to use it to house a full-time forester. This was a ridiculous condition, because the property had less than thirteen acres of trees. The Dodds were never notified of the zoning change, even though they

---

2. Pacific Legal Foundation Release, 14 March 1996.

continued to receive property tax bills for the forty acres of land.

Unable to build their home, the Dodds tried to sell the acreage to timber interests. But twenty-two acres of the property are covered by soil that won't support forest vegetation. Of the remaining eighteen acres, only 12.6 are currently forested. The rest is subject to severe erosion because of steep slopes. In other words, the land is completely and utterly unsuitable for forestry. The value of the land as currently zoned is less than $700—and that's if you don't figure in the costs of property taxes.

Lois Jemtegaard

A nearly identical episode happened to Lois Jemtegaard of Skamania County, Washington. She owns a vacant twenty-acre parcel zoned for a single-family home. Jemtegaard wanted to sell the property and use the money to fix her current home, which she says is "is literally falling down around my ears." Under the federal Columbia River Gorge National Scenic Area Act, her land may only be used for agriculture or timber operations. But Jemtegaard ran into the same problems as the Dodds.

The property is not suitable for farming because of its small size, the bad weather, and the fact that there is a 700-foot-deep box canyon in the middle of it. While the soils will technically support timber production, only about five acres of the parcel are now wooded. This is also too small to harvest economically. No problem, said the Columbia River Gorge Commission. Jemtegaard's soil will support growth of 170 cubic feet of wood fiber per acre per year. All she has to do is wait *65 years* for harvestable timber.

The most frustrating thing about zoning laws is that government is perfectly willing to take both sides against the middle—property owners. When four residents of Bakersfield, California, filed suit to prevent the opening of a boarding facility for mentally retarded adults because it violated local zoning restrictions, they were sued in turn by the U.S. Department of Housing and Urban Development (HUD) for violating housing discrimination laws. "The government is arguing that anyone who defends their property rights must be a bigot," said Victor Wolski, the residents' attorney. HUD also slapped a lawsuit against residents of Berkeley, California, who protested the placement of a homeless shelter and halfway house in their neighborhood.

HANDICAPPING COMMON SENSE

These are but a bare few of the many examples of restrictions that government agencies place on property. Other agencies regulate what products businesses may use, whom they may hire, what kind of vehicles they may buy, and on and on. The Americans with Disabilities Act places enormous, often arbitrary, restrictions on property rights. In one instance that received major media play, the Odd Ball Cabaret, a striptease club in Los Angeles, was forced to remove a shower stall from its stage. The city ruled that the shower (used as part of the show) was not accessible to the disabled. Another strip club in Bellevue, Washington, was cited for lacking a wheelchair lift to the stage for disabled performers. Naturally, the club has no disabled performers and is unlikely to hire any in the future.

The Federal Highway Commission proposed a special waiver program in 1994 so that truck drivers could still drive even though they were blind in one eye and had weak vision in the other. Perhaps then they could make use of the Braille instructions the federal government required banks to place on each drive-through automated teller machine. Burger King settled a lawsuit by agreeing to install visual electronic ordering devices at ten restaurants to accommodate deaf customers at their drive-through windows.

RECYCLED REASONING

Recycling laws further restrict property rights. Many states now mandate a specific content of recycled material in many products—whether or not these mandates make any sense or are economical. As the *Wall Street Journal* reported in January 1995: "At least by any practical, short-term measure, curbside recycling doesn't pay. It costs residents and local governments hundreds of millions of dollars more than can be recouped by selling the sorted trash. It requires huge new fleets of collections trucks that add to traffic congestion and pollution. And it does so at a time when landfill space turns out to be both plentiful and extremely cheap."

Recycled and virgin goods are no different from any other commodity. They are ruled by the laws of supply and demand. For example, let's replace "recycled goods" and "virgin goods" with "tea" and "coffee." The infringement on property rights (and freedom of choice) quickly becomes clear. Suppose the government decided that tea was better than coffee. Suppose it applied a surcharge on the sale of coffee and used the money to subsidize the sale of tea. It would create a Division of Tea that would promote the benefits of tea and the disadvantages of coffee. It would require cafés and supermarkets to stock more tea than coffee. It would send money to tea producers, tea processors, and tea sellers to offset the unprofitability of their businesses.

Suppose that despite all these efforts, citizens continued to drink more coffee than tea because a) they preferred it; and b) coffee remained much cheaper than tea. Would Americans allow the gov-

125

ernment to expand the Division of Tea and use tax money to create "tea market development zones?"

The preponderance of recycling programs has led to a glut of materials. This has driven the price for recycled materials down. It doesn't take a rocket scientist to see that if you spend $100 per ton recycling something, and can only sell it for $5 per ton, you are not going to be in business very long. Unless the government is involved, that is. What happens then is that the government charges someone else (taxes on citizens, fees on businesses) $95 for each ton of material recycled. The process then magically "breaks even"—except that there is now $95 fewer in the pocket of a consumer or on the payroll of the business. "Recycling as a government-mandated, garbage-management concept has largely failed," said Patricia Poore, editor of *Garbage* magazine.[3]

In California, the state-managed recycling system is a train wreck waiting to happen. The entire project—processing subsidies, grants, advertising, and rebates—is funded by people *not recycling*. Those people never reclaim the fee added to beverage purchases. This unclaimed deposit keeps the unprofitable system running. If California's program were successful in getting everyone to recycle, it would go bankrupt and the whole system would collapse. Meanwhile, as recycling grows, the state system is *expanding*. Since recycling only occurs when the goods are resold in the marketplace, the next step is to subsidize businesses to purchase recycled goods (this is already occurring) or force them to do so.

In many localities, private citizens and businesses are required to sort their trash or face fines. The recycling propaganda has worked so well that cities are feeling the backlash. Suddenly, recycling "scavengers" are a law enforcement concern. Los Angeles and other cities have begun to impose tough penalties on scavengers, including fines

---

3. See "Is Recycling Succeeding?" by Bill Breen, *Garbage,* July 1993, p. 36ff.

and even jail time. Police are setting up citizen hot lines and im-
pounding cars. City officials want to spend $600,000 in recycling
revenues to expand anti-scavenging police patrols throughout Los
Angeles and build recycling bins that can be locked.

This is not to suggest that recycling is a bad thing. But once again
we see government losing sight of its goal (reducing waste) while
redoubling its efforts (wasting tax dollars). Recycling mandates are
one of the enforcement mechanisms by which property use is restricted—even to the possible detriment of the environment. In
many states, governments have mandated recycled content for
newsprint. This leads to increased energy usage, increased sulfur
dioxide emissions, and could lead to *fewer* trees being planted by
America's timber companies.

OTHER MANDATES

In California, a mandate was passed requiring that 2 percent of the
vehicles sold in the state by 1998 emit "zero emissions." The problem is that electric vehicles are still much more expensive than gas-
powered vehicles. A battery pack can cost $10,000 by itself and must
be replaced after several years of use. Most electric vehicles have
about a 100-mile range, which is reduced by the use of heaters, wind-
shield wipers, radios, defrosters, etc. No one has explained what you
are supposed to do if you have a late-night emergency and your
electric car is still recharging. Or how an electric car will start in the
cold weather near Mount Shasta.

Federal Occupational Safety and Health Administration regula-
tors recently halved the permissible exposure to airborne asbestos.
OSHA will now *presume* that certain types of materials are asbestos.
"It's going to impose a lot of compliance costs on people to treat as
asbestos material that really isn't," said attorney Donald C. Nanney.
Any thermal system insulation and surfacing material found in build-

ings constructed before 1980 will be presumed to contain asbestos. Surfacing material is defined as anything that is sprayed, troweled on, or otherwise applied to surfaces for acoustical, fireproofing, and other purposes. Building owners also are required to maintain, for the duration of ownership, records regarding the identification, location, and quantity of known or presumed asbestos in their buildings, as well as all notifications given and received. The records would have to be kept *in perpetuity* and transferred to subsequent owners. Where will a property owner find space to store these records?

The death rates for high school football are anywhere from 100 to 2,000 times higher than death from asbestos in school buildings. Children are from 2,700 to 54,000 times more likely to drown than to die from asbestos. Yet building owners are spending fortunes removing asbestos from buildings—despite evidence that disturbing it is more harmful to health than leaving it alone.

When the Equal Employment Opportunity Commission (EEOC) ruled that the "Hooters" restaurant chain had to hire male waiters, conduct "sensitivity training," and establish a scholarship fund to enhance job opportunities for men, the corporation defied the ruling and took out full-page newspaper ads advising the regulators to "Get a Grip." The women who worked at Hooters protested that the EEOC decision would put them out of work. Federal regulations of workplace behavior have put more than one restaurant out of business. Sarah J. McCarthy, co-owner of Amel's Restaurant in Pittsburgh, described how federal sexual harassment laws can have unintended consequences: "I attended a sexual harassment trial involving a sports bar where songs like 'If I Only Had A Brain' from the *Wizard of Oz* were thought by the bartender to be all in fun. Singing that song in front of a waitress was considered in court evidence of a hostile environment. . . . The alleged harassment, which the owner knew nothing about, resulted in legal costs and fines of over $500,000. The owner was guilty by what is known in the law as the 'should-have-known standard,' which states that any employer should have known of everything that occurred in his business. In the end, the bar closed and eighty people lost their jobs, which many testified were the best jobs they ever had."

McCarthy described the current climate between businesses and government regulators this way: "Business owners are nervous these days. Like citizens of a police state, we wait for a knock on the door. Wendy's thinks it's too risky to sell hot chocolate in America. The Russian Tea Room in New York City no longer sells steak tartare. The Las Vegas Hilton was fined $7 million for not recognizing that the partying pilots of Tailhook needed a baby-sitter. . . . It makes you think it's time to move somewhere business-friendly—maybe to China or Iran."

Infringements on private property rights by government agencies are endless. For every agency at every level of jurisdiction there are stories of citizens and businesses who have been wronged. Those listed here are only a small representation. I could go on and describe the damages done by asset forfeiture laws, rent control, racial quota mandates, and the Internal Revenue Code.

It may already be too late to warn of a "slippery slope." Can government get much more intrusive? The U.S. Supreme Court, in *Fleming v. Nestor* (1960), ruled that American citizens have no legal claim to future Social Security benefits, even though they have paid into a "trust fund" their entire lives. An item published in the *Wall Street Journal* informed us that you may be committing a federal crime if you use overnight shipping services, such as Federal Express. A little-known law requires that your shipment must be considered "urgent" or you must use the U.S. Postal Service. Federal postal inspectors recently visited an Atlanta credit reporting agency and found that it was using overnight services for "non-urgent" mail. The government fined the company $30,000, the amount the Postal Service would have collected if the materials had been sent first-class. Under the same law, GTE was fined $312,000 for what the Postal Service calls "recovered" revenue.

Who benefits from all this government intrusiveness? Who benefits from the denial of your constitutionally guaranteed, God-given property rights? The answer can be found by examining the people and organizations that draft and enforce the laws for endangered species, wetlands, wildlife preservation, expansion of public lands, recycling, trails, easements, etc. I refer to them as the eco-federal coalition.

8

THE ECO-FEDERAL COALITION

"How do you say to somebody, 'No, I don't want you to have your job.'"

—DEBRA CALLAHAN, DIRECTOR OF THE W. ALTON JONES
FOUNDATION'S ENVIRONMENTAL GRASS ROOTS PROGRAM

A radical environmental agenda is being carried out every day in the
United States by a group of committed activists I have termed the
eco-federal coalition. Their philosophy is elitist, rooted in the belief that the average American, if left to his or her own devices, would
surely perform the most stupid and harmful actions possible to the
environment. Thus, the average American must be restrained by
regulations and, if necessary, removed from his or her own land.
Such a philosophy requires that more and more property be brought
under the day-to-day control of the coalition. This is already happening.

I am not claiming that there is a cabal of federal workers and environmental activists meeting in smoke-filled rooms plotting the
takeover of the United States. This is not a conspiracy. It is a coali-

tion of government agencies and nonprofit groups who share the same systematic view of managing land and the environment. They agree in principle as to what steps are necessary, as they see it, to prevent wholesale eco-disaster. And so, more often than not, they work together to bring those changes about.

How can bureaucrats in a government agency and environmental activists agree so completely about goals and methods? Aren't they from completely different ends of the social, political, and cultural spectrum? The simple answer is that the eco-federal coalition exists because its members are *not* two separate groups of people, but are often the same people. There is a revolving door between federal government regulatory agencies and private environmental organizations that is constantly spinning. Executives from private groups are appointed to government agencies, serve their terms, and are re-hired as executives by other private groups. Not only do coalition members know each other, but they have often worked side by side.

If you think this an exaggeration, here is just a partial list of high-ranking government employees and high-ranking officials in environmental organizations, with their present and previous affiliations specified:

- Bruce Babbitt: Secretary of the Interior—President of the League of Conservation Voters.
- Carol Browner: Administrator, Environmental Protection Agency—Attorney for Citizen Action.
- George Frampton: Assistant Secretary of Fish, Wildlife and Parks of the U.S. Department of the Interior—President of The Wilderness Society.
- David Gardiner: Assistant Administrator for Policy Planning and Evaluation at the Environmental Protection Agency— Legislative Director for the Sierra Club.
- Jay Hair: Executive Director, National Wildlife Federation—

Member of the Environmental Protection Agency's Biotechnology Science Coordinating Committee.
- Frank Lovejoy: Scientific Advisor, U.S. Department of the Interior—Vice President for Science for World Wide Fund for Nature.
- Jessica Tuchman Matthews: Deputy Undersecretary of State for Global Affairs—Vice President of the World Resources Institute.
- Roger E. McManus: President, Center for Marine Conservation—Member of the President's Council on Environmental Quality.
- Jean Nelson: General Counsel, Environmental Protection Agency—Member of the executive committee of the Southern Environmental Law Center.
- Hazel Rollins O'Leary: Secretary of Energy—Vice Chair of the board of directors of The Keystone Center.
- Rafe Pomerance: Deputy Assistant Secretary of State for Environment, Health and Natural Resources—Senior Associate for Policy Affairs at the World Resource Institute.
- Dan W. Reicher: Attorney, Natural Resources Defense Council—Member of President's Council on Environmental Quality.
- William Reilly: former Environmental Protection Agency Administrator—President of The Conservation Foundation.
- Alice Rivlin: Deputy Director, U.S. Office of Management and Budget—Member of the governing council of the Wilderness Society.
- Rodger Schlickeisen: President, Defenders of Wildlife—Associate Director for Economics and Administration for the U.S. Office of Management and Budget.
- Gus Speth: Director of United Nations Development Programme—President of the World Resource Institute.

- Russell Train: Chairman, World Wildlife Fund—Administrator for the Environmental Protection Agency.
- Brooks Yeager: Director, Office of Policy Analysis, U.S. Department of the Interior—Vice President of governmental relations for the National Audubon Society.

The revolving door prize must go to Douglas Wheeler, who is currently the Secretary for Resources for the state of California. Wheeler previously worked for the World Wildlife Fund, the Conservation Foundation, the Sierra Club, the American Farmland Trust, and the National Trust for Historic Preservation, as well as serving a stint as Deputy Assistant Secretary of the Interior.

These are well-paying positions, with substantial benefits and perks. Jay Hair, the president of the National Wildlife Federation, made $232,640 in 1994. John Sawhill, president of the Nature Conservancy, makes $185,000 per year, as does Kathryn Fuller, executive director of the World Wildlife Fund. Peter Berle, president of the National Audubon Society, makes $178,000.

It requires a healthy income to support a truly green lifestyle. Surain afSandeberg is the financial manager for the Nature Conservancy of Washington State. She and her husband, Robert, bought a houseboat for $177,500, then spent over $300,000 to renovate it. The houseboat has a lovely view of the Seattle skyline and contains all the "environmentally correct" conveniences: composition board-siding, bamboo floors, an ambient wine cellar, sculpted drain spouts, a metal roof, and bog plants. The kitchen counter is made of tambrin, a teaklike wood grown in Central America, and the pantry doors are hand-painted with scenes from the afSandebergs' life. Oh, and it has a hot tub.

William Arthur is the northwest regional director of the Sierra Club. He has been outspoken in his remarks against the timber industry. "We cut like there's no tomorrow, and tomorrow caught up with us yesterday," he told a forestry panel in Portland. But when he needed some cash to repair his vacation home, Arthur cleared 70 percent of the standing timber on his own land. He left the minimum number of trees necessary to meet state requirements: two wildlife trees, two "recruitment trees" to spur new growth and a couple of downed logs per acre. Arthur collected about $10,000 from the sale. The Sierra Club urges private landowners to restrict their harvests to 10 to 20 percent of the total volume. "If I owned a chunk of land, 70 to 80 percent would be excessive," said a Sierra Club spokesman.

Arthur is perfectly free to cut down his timber for cash to repair his vacation home or for any other purpose. The problem is that organizations like the one for which he works wants to prevent other landowners from doing the same. And Arthur is not an aberration. The Nature Conservancy manages oil drilling and production on several preserves. The National Audobon Society has drilled thirty-seven wells in the Paul J. Rainey Wilderness Sanctuary in Louisiana. The group's efforts have produced one successful crude oil well, and fifteen successful natural gas wells. The group earns $2 million annually from these wells. Drilling has also occurred in the Corkscrew Swamp Sanctuary near Naples, Florida, and the Bernard Baker Sanctuary in Michigan.[1]

ECO-ACTIVISTS: WHO ARE THEY?

Timber interests? Oil wells? But aren't environmentalists simple nature lovers, hikers, and New Age ex-hippies? Some are, but the demographics of officials of environmental organizations might surprise you. Professors Stanley Rothman and S. Robert Lichter recently surveyed one hundred individuals chosen randomly from the

---

1. *Wall Street Journal,* editorial by Jane Shaw and Pam Snyder, 7 September 1995, and response from National Audubon Society president John Flicker, 18 September 1995.

senior staffs and boards of directors of mainstream environmental groups. They were four times likelier than the general public to have a family income over $75,000. Ironically, only 6 percent of them agreed that government regulation of business generally does more harm than good (among the general populace, *ten times* as many people—61 percent—agreed with that statement). A New York market research firm discovered in 1982 that environmentalists were most likely to be white, urban dwellers with more than one college degree and a service industry job. Nearly 88 percent of those on the Sierra Club's mailing list hold professional managerial jobs and the list's median household income is above $40,000. Members of environmental groups comprise a tiny minority. Only about 5 percent of Americans belong to an environmental group of any kind.

The government side of the eco-federal coalition is also well-situated. The Environmental Protection Agency's budget has increased eightfold since 1972. The most recent budget request made by President Clinton for EPA was $7.2 billion, an 8 percent boost with enough funding for 800 new federal employees. The number of regulators and the budget at the U.S. Fish and Wildlife Service has doubled since 1985. And nothing is so permanent as the job of a federal regulator. In the 1994 fiscal year, less than 0.0015 percent of the federal workforce were let go due to misconduct or poor performance. In fact, federal environmental officials enjoy many of the same amenities as their private counterparts. The Inspector General for the General Services Administration released a report in October 1995, stating that the cost of federal construction is inflated by amenities that tenants insist the GSA add.

The money for federal officials, of course, comes out of the taxpayers' pockets. But you may be surprised to know that quite a bit of the private organizations' money also comes from the taxpayers' pockets. What is worse, many groups receive tax funds, then are

The Eco-Federal Coalition

allowed to lobby Congress for more. The World Wildlife Fund, for example, receives $7 million annually from the federal government. Other organizations receive different forms of federal largesse.

The Appalachian Mountain Club is permitted to run a recreational facility in New Hampshire's White Mountain National Forest. The U.S. Forest Service allows the club to derive $3.5 million in revenues from free use of federal land. The group then lobbies for federal land purchases. According to Alliance for America, a property rights group in Caroga Lake, New York, an internal memo from the group's annual meeting with the U.S. Forest Service contains this sentence: "We need to be more coordinated in our interests so that AMC's high regard in Washington can be used to lobby for funding for forest needs as identified by USFS staff, for whom lobbying is prohibited."[2]

Environmental groups receive mountains of money through lawsuits. Cooperative judges are more than happy to sentence businesses convicted of polluting or filling in wetlands to pay environmental groups. Why a private advocacy organization like the Sierra Club should benefit financially when a corporation is convicted of polluting has never been adequately explained. Federal law allows groups to file "citizen action suits" under the Clean Water Act, Clean Air Act, the Resource Conservation Recovery Act, Superfund, the Safe Drinking Water Act, and the Endangered Species Act. Settlements often require cash bonuses to advocacy groups as well. In a Clean Water Act case settlement, a Tennessee defendant paid a $1.25 million settlement, of which all but $125,000 went to the Tennessee Environmental Endowment. Coors Brewing signed a 1991 agreement to avert a Sierra Club lawsuit by contributing $160,000 to the Trust for Public Land. Yet another lawsuit required Bethlehem Steel to contribute $50,000 to Save Our Streams, $100,000 to

2. Alliance for America press release, 8 November 1995.

137

the National Fish and Wildlife Federation, $200,000 to the Trust for Public Land. Standard and Poor's Ratings Group released a report that estimated insurers' total exposure to environmental claims at $40 billion. No one is safe from these legal actions. The Sierra Club filed a lawsuit to prevent construction of a hospice for terminally ill patients in Monterey, California, because of an alleged small native pine forest.

FUNDRAISING

Environmental groups also do a lot of direct-mail fundraising. Junk mail such as the following is the meat and potatoes of the coalition:

> "(Representative Young) has personally sworn to destroy the ESA!"
> "Please rush your check today.
> —Defenders of Wildlife

> ". . . the predicted sentence for hundreds of species—if our opponents get their way—is **EXTINCTION!** I'm asking you to sit down right now and please make out the most generous contribution you can to this vital effort."
> —Sierra Club

People who seek to reform environmental laws or who stand in support of property rights are painted as demons, who can only be held at bay by your generous contributions. Even I have uses to the eco-federal coalition. "Given the burning hatred Representative Pombo has always expressed towards the ESA, his bill is likely to be . . . the harshest attack yet on endangered species," reads a fund-raising letter for the National Wildlife Federation.

Environmental groups are not the grassroots organizations they would have you believe. They are huge corporations. The largest of them—and the largest threat to the rights of private property owners—are the conservancies.

LAND TRUSTS AND CONSERVANCIES

The Nature Conservancy (TNC) is the largest, wealthiest environmental organization in the United States. Its mission is to protect land that contains rare or endangered animals or plants. Since its founding in 1951, The Nature Conservancy has set aside more than 6.3 million acres in the United States and Canada. It currently owns or controls at least 2.8 million acres. While by far the biggest, TNC is not the only "land trust" in America. There are more than 900 of them.

The question you may be asking yourself is: "If the group has bought over 6 million acres of land in its history, and now owns less than 3 million acres, what happened to the rest of the land?" The answer is simple, and one of the greatest scandals of the conservation movement. The majority of the land purchased by land trusts is resold, at huge profits, to the federal government. In their invaluable book, *Trashing the Economy,* Ron Arnold and Alan Gottlieb inform us that "TNC's ledgers showed that as of June 30, 1990, it was holding $53.5 million in land 'for resale to the government.' TNC's ledgers showed that they received $90,693,000 from sales of land to government agencies in 1992."[3] TNC added more than $78 million in sales to that in 1995.

The process is uncomplicated. While the federal government's appetite for land is insatiable, it often finds resistance from property owners. Many do not want their land turned into a national park or

---

3. *Trashing the Economy: How Runaway Environmentalism Is Wrecking America,* by Ron Arnold and Alan Gottlieb, Free Enterprise Press, 1993, p. 89.

subject to restrictive federal regulations, so they refuse to sell to the government. Also, government agencies often have property on their "wish lists" that they cannot buy because they haven't wrung it out of American taxpayers yet. This is where land trusts like The Nature Conservancy come in. The trusts offer to buy the property, or sometimes they set up front organizations to make the offer. The owner sells the land (often at a greatly reduced price because he or she receives a substantial tax deduction for doing so), the trust marks it up to the "fair market value" price, and then sells it to the federal government. A spokesman for The Nature Conservancy admitted that nearly 90 percent of the land bought by the TNC in Texas ended up in federal hands. What it cannot sell immediately to the government, the conservancies will exploit in some way. It is not unusual for such groups to build housing developments, plantations, and farms. In the language of environmentalism, such organizations are called "conservancies" or "land trusts." In the real world, we call these groups by a name which describes their actual function—real estate firms. How many people would send their hard-earned $25 donations to a $275-million-dollar real estate firm?

No one is speculating or guessing that this is going on. Arnold and Gottlieb uncovered a Memorandum of Understanding between TNC and the Bureau of Land Management dated 23 March 1990. It says: "TNC has the experience and capability to assist the BLM in the acquisition of privately owned lands."[4] Columnist Tony Snow calls this practice "green feudalism," and it is an appropriate description. The eco-federal coalition gets as fat as medieval barons while the serfs give up all they have to support the system. William Perry Pendley, president of the Mountain States Legal Foundation, describes the multiple ways taxpayers are shanghaied into supporting this corrupt practice:

---

4. Ibid. p. 95.

"First, the property owner takes a tax deduction for the difference between the selling price and the fair market value.
Second, the land agent sells the land to the government at
its 'fair market value.' Third, the land agent is paid for
'costs' and 'expenses,' which the inspector general faults as
excessive, unnecessary, or even illegal. Fourth, the land
agent is typically a nonprofit, public interest entity that pays
no taxes on its multimillion-dollar enterprise. Fifth, the
lands, now in the hands of the government, are off the tax
rolls of the typically hard-pressed local government. Sixth,
the purchased lands, once in productive use and generating
income (multiplied through the local economy), now lie fallow. Seventh, the government will be asked to make federal 'payments in lieu of taxes' as a small recompense to the
local government that has now less productive income—and
tax-generating private property."[5]

The effects are multiplied throughout public policy. Environmental
groups are among the most zealous opponents of a cut in the capital gains tax rate. Why? Because high capital gains tax rates provide
incentives to landowners to deal with land trusts. It works this way:
Top income bracket landowners are unwilling to sell their property,
particularly in California, because they would face a 28 percent federal capital gains tax, and 11 percent state capital gains tax, and 6
percent in commissions and fees. But if they sell at about a 25 percent discount to an environmental organization, the after-tax gain
will be almost the same.

A change made to the U.S. tax laws in 1993 also allows individuals who are subject to the alternate minimum tax to deduct the
full market value of their land if they donate it to conservation

5. *War on the West: Government Tyranny on America's Great Frontier,* by William Perry Pendley, Regnery, 1995, pp. 112–113.

groups. Entertainer Barbra Streisand (who, coincidentally, has her own $4 million environmental foundation) donated her twenty-acre, $15-million Malibu ranch to the Santa Monica Mountains Conservancy. The deal closed on 31 December 1993, the last day of the tax year. Unfortunately for the citizens of Malibu, they were saddled with utility and maintenance costs for the property for two years. Upkeep on the four houses, five bridges, tennis court, and private screening room cost Malibu taxpayers more than $50,000 per year.

"There are three distinct financial advantages for making such gifts: avoiding capital gains, getting a deduction for the full market value of the gift and avoiding the costs of selling the property," says Martin Rosen, president of the Trust for Public Land. The trust can then sell the land to the government for full value. This sale is *exempt* from capital gains taxes and the conservancy turns a huge profit, sometimes within minutes.

The late columnist Warren Brookes described one such instance involving the Trust for Public Land. The trust bought property in the town of Wyeth, Oregon, to be included in Mount Hood National Forest. "TPL was well rewarded," Brookes wrote. "It bought these properties from Joseph Yoerger in two blocks. In the first, it paid a purchase price of $750,000 on August 14, 1980, at 11:22 A.M. At 11:23 A.M., TPL sold this block to the Forest Service for $944,000, a gain of $194,000. Three minutes later, TPL executed its option to purchase the second Yoerger block for $175,000, and one minute later sold it to the Forest Service for $292,000, a gain of $117,000 on a $1,000 option."

Some sellers, feeling they had been hoodwinked, began to fight back. In 1975, Dr. Claude Moore donated a 357-acre conservation sanctuary in Virginia to the National Wildlife Federation. In 1986, NWF decided it needed a $40 million seven-story building in Washington, DC, more than it needed the sanctuary. It sold Dr. Moore's land to a developer who wanted to put 1,350 housing units on the site. Dr. Moore sued. He lost.

MEDIA COMPLICITY

Haven't you heard about these cases? Didn't you know that environmentalism is Big Business? Of course you didn't, because the press is too busy accepting every claim of these organizations at face value. The watchdog press is more like the lapdog press when it comes to the eco-federal coalition. There is a Society of Environmental Journalists, ostensibly a professional organization for reporters covering the environmental beat, which follows the green party line exclusively. Kevin Carmody, health and environmental writer for the *Daily Southtown* in Chicago and founding board member of the Society of Environmental Journalists, showed his journalistic objectivity when he wrote: "Some of the armed militias that are sprouting throughout the country have shown anti-environmentalist leanings. Endangered species, including seals and owls, are being intentionally hunted down by those who oppose the law protecting them." For this outrageous accusation, Carmody—in the best tradition of today's green journalism—offers no substantiation. When Robert Kahn, city editor of the *Bakersfield Californian,* heard the story of Cindy Domenigoni and her experiences with the Kangaroo rat, he wrote: "For Domenigoni to whine about 'losing' 800 of the thousands of acres her family wrested from the Indians, because the federal government wishes to protect plants and animals, compounds hypocrisy and amnesia to the point of lunacy."[6]

These headlines flashed across America's newspapers when cuts were proposed to appropriations for the Environmental Protection

---

6. "Nutcake Haynes Reveals Diabolic 'Plot,'" *Bakersfield Californian,* 1 May 1995.

143

Agency in order to balance the federal budget. Remember, the EPA's budget has increased *eightfold* since 1972:

"EPA Vital to Health, Environment of Maine"
—*Maine Sunday Telegram*
"Dirty Environment Guaranteed"—*The Kansas City Star*
"Polluted Fish, Polluted Legislation"—*The New York Times*
"Bad Times for the Environment"—*Hartford Courant*
"Don't Emasculate EPA"—*The Oregonian*
"Slashing EPA Budget Will Cost Us"—*Kennebec Journal* (Maine)
"House Tries to Slip EPA Poison Pill in Funds Bill"
—*The Salt Lake Tribune*
"Coming from Congress: Dirty Water, Foul Air"
—*Oakland Tribune*
"As GOP Wolves Circle, EPA Girds for a Fight"—*Rocky Mountain News*

Such advocacy is not limited to small and mid-size dailies. The *New York Times,* for example, has already come out in favor of subverting private property rights. A harsh exaggeration? When a mine was proposed at Henderson Mountain, three miles from Yellowstone National Park, the *Times* suggested that, since Congress was unlikely to take steps to stop the mine, President Clinton and his administrative agencies should exercise their regulatory powers to make it "onerous" for the company to proceed with its plans.

WHO FUNDS THE GREENS?

Many people have told me that it takes an eco-federal coalition (plus the press) to fight against Big Business. Greedy capitalists are standing in line, anxiously awaiting opportunities to plunder our natural resources in their relentless pursuit of profit. Only dedicated environmentalists and government regulators can save the planet for our children and grandchildren against the depredations of huge corporations. There is a serious problem with this theory. Big Business is, by far, the largest financial supporter of the eco-federal coalition.

It often makes me laugh out loud when I hear property rights organizations described as "tools of Big Business." I would like to compare the office of Jay Hair, president of the National Wildlife Federation, to that of Peggy Reigle, chairman of the Fairness to Land Owners Committee. Hundreds of property rights organizations are run out of people's garages. Can the Sierra Club make the same claim?

Besides having the biggest ally of all—the federal government— environmental groups receive funding from these "mom and pop" companies: Anheuser Busch, Apple Computers, Archer Daniels Midland, ARCO, Ashland Oil, British Petroleum, Burlington Northern, Chevron, Coca Cola, Conoco, Dow, DuPont, Exxon, Ford, GTE, Hearst, Kellogg, Mars, Marshall & Marshall Lumber, Miller Brewing, Mobil Oil, Monsanto, Morgan Guaranty Trust, Mutual of Omaha, Pennzoil, Philip Morris, Phillips Petroleum, Procter & Gamble, Rockefeller, Shell Oil, 3M, Timberland, Union Pacific, USX, Wells Fargo, and Weyerhauser. . . . This is only a partial list, mind you.

What? You didn't know environmental groups accepted money from oil companies, timber companies, chemical companies, and mining companies? You didn't know they accepted money from the corporate elites such as Hearst, Morgan, and Rockefeller? You didn't know they accepted money from Philip Morris, the tobacco giant? Perhaps the reason you don't know is because the "newspapers of record" also donate heavily to environmental organizations. These include the *New York Times,* the *Washington Post,* and Times Mirror

Corporation (the publishers of the *Los Angeles Times*). So much for objective reporting.

It doesn't seem to make sense for environmental groups to put out of business the very people who are bankrolling them. Nor does it seem to make sense for large corporations to finance the very people who are seeking to put them out of business. But the dirty little secret of the eco-federal coalition is that it simply wants to milk these corporations just as it milks the taxpayers. Its members know that Exxon and Dow Chemical will simply pass the costs of environmental regulations and lawsuits down to the consumer. The "green" that interests the big environmental organizations is not the kind found in the forest, but in the wallet.

Why do big corporations allow themselves to be milked? Primarily for three reasons. Number one: Sometimes it is easier and cheaper just to pay "protection." Make large enough donations to the cause, and the cause won't target you for lawsuits and no-notice inspections. "Since we are good neighbors," said DuPont's Megan Burns, "we are allowed to continue making products." I don't know what you would call it when green groups "allow" DuPont to continue making products, but the word "extortion" does come to mind. Number two: Sometimes it is profitable. When the Rockefellers donated land to create and expand national parks in Wyoming, it greatly increased the value of the surrounding land which they owned, but did not donate. High-priced resorts bring in more cash than shacks in the wilderness. The publicity generated for being "environmentally correct" doesn't hurt, either. Number three: Sometimes it drives competitors out of business. Let's face it. Coca Cola, Archer Daniels Midland, and 3M can afford to spend millions of dollars defending lawsuits and bribing environmental groups. But smaller companies cannot. They simply go out of business when faced with strangling restrictions on their property. The rich, as they are wont to do, get richer.

ENVIRONMENTAL ELITISM

The fact that the eco-federal coalition works so closely and so well with the corporate elite should come as no surprise. The philosophy of the environmental movement regarding property rights is fundamentally elitist. Their creed is: *You're destroying the planet, you moron. We must save you from yourself.*

"The politics of the West are now best understood in terms which are not political but psychological," editorialized John Margolis, syndicated columnist for the *Chicago Tribune*. "The West as an entity, and (with some exceptions) Western men as individuals are cases of arrested development. All this talk about frontier ethics, property rights, state sovereignty and 'wise use' is merely a disguise for what the West and the Westerners are really saying: 'Waaaaaahhh!' "

You can't take care of yourself, you big baby. Big Green Brother will watch out for you.

James L. Pierce is a specialist in takings claims and environmental law in San Francisco, California. He writes: "The day is here when we must view our open lands as refuges of biodiversity and places to maintain some balance between humanity and the rest of the planet. Our physical environment is a gift to sustain us and the rest of earth's life forms. It is not something to be squandered or spent with finality. It is not solely ours to spend; it belongs to our children's children, and their children, and to other species." Unfortunately, Mr. Pierce and other defenders of "our collective property rights" are never around when the property taxes are due, or when a fire or flood destroys acreage, or when the presence of an endangered species drives an owner into bankruptcy. What Pierce and his friends want is for *them* to decide how to use *your* land, and for *you* to pay for it.

Carl Pope, executive director of the Sierra Club, had this to say about property rights: "Land was, and always has been, infused with a public trust. Kings and Congress, when they awarded ownership of land, retained the right to protect the surrounding community by regulating the use of that land in the public interest. . . . [A landowner's] use of land could not constitute a nuisance for his neighbors, and was subject to a wide range of restrictions by the state and local governments—indeed, the only right he clearly and unequivocally enjoyed was the right to occupy his property and to keep others from occupying it—so long as it did not impinge on access to waterways, traditional rights of way, trails and roads, wetlands and beaches, and on and on. . . . But 300 million Americans driving Ford Broncos eating at McDonald's and aspiring to a modest approximation of O. J. Simpson's house, must pay the price of their wealth and numbers. They cannot live as unconstrained as frontier Americans. . . . It is no accident that the property rights movement overlaps so heavily with the members of the militia and other advocates of establishing public order on the basis of an armed populace, with justice flowing to the fastest draw. . . ."[7]

What a fascinating collection of sentences! First, according to Pope, you don't own your land, the king or Congress does. They will let you continue to use it as long as you are not a "nuisance." (How is that for paternalism?) You only have *one clear and unequivocal right,* according to Pope, to occupy the property and keep others from occupying it . . . *unless* it impinges on access to "wetlands and beaches, and on and on. . . ." Pope should look up the word "unequivocal" in the dictionary. Now we get to the meat of the matter. If you drive a Ford Bronco, eat at McDonald's, and *aspire* to live in

---

7. From a speech to the Commonwealth Club, San Francisco, CA, on 31 June 1995.

a mansion, then *you're the problem!* Mr. Pope, we may assume, lives in a dirt hovel, walks to his office (also a dirt hovel), eats berries and twigs, and chisels his editorials into stone tablets. Pope then finishes with a flourish, opining that property rights activists are gun-toting kooks, just waiting for the next quick draw. You are not only the problem, *you're dangerous!* Thank God the Sierra Club is here to defend the U.S.A. Send your most generous contribution today.

You don't have to take my word for it. Alexander Cockburn and Jeffrey St. Clair, contributing editors to *The Nation,* described in an article for *Wild Forest Review* why the property rights movement has made such large strides. "The mainstream environmental movement was elitist, highly paid, detached from the people, indifferent to the working class, and a firm ally of big government. . . . The environmental movement is now accurately perceived as just another well-financed and cynical special interest group, its rancid infrastructure supported by Democratic Party operatives and millions in grants from corporate foundations."

The central planners, discredited in virtually every country on Earth, thrive in the eco-federal coalition. They oppose the Tenth Amendment because it undermines their power. Imagine if the Sierra Club and the Natural Resources Defense Council had to compete for time at local town halls and public hearings. The hearings I chaired for the House Task Force showed that they would get short shrift. It is much easier by far to go see your old coworkers at the EPA and the FWS in Washington, DC, and get them to do your dirty work without getting your designer suit messed up with "grassroots."

IDEOLOGICAL ROOTS

Throughout history there have been groups of motivated people who sought to consolidate political power for themselves and for like-minded followers. The vehicles they used to achieve this power differed wildly, running the entire gamut from religion to communism. What they shared is a distrust for the individual. In recent times, this distrust has been manifested by opposition to the capitalist economic system, which, in the view of central planners, is too chaotic, leading to unequal distribution of resources and wealth. The loss of individual liberty that is required to bring this "chaos" to order is a necessary price to pay, in their view.

The means they use to control property are sometimes moderate and sometimes extreme. They borrow ideas equally from fascists, anarchists, globalists, and communists. Officials from the U.S. Department of the Interior went to the World Heritage Centre of the United National Education, Scientific and Cultural Organization (UNESCO) and asked its officials to place Yellowstone National Park on an international "Endangered Heritage List." When UNESCO said it couldn't afford to undertake the mission, the Interior Department offered to pay for it (with your tax dollars, of course).

They will use "eco-spies" to control property. The Environmental Protection Agency funds a program of "volunteer monitors." Groups of monitors (133 of them at last count) look for "violators" whom they report or sue. A volunteer pilots' organization called LightHawk takes to the air to monitor timber activities from Alaska to Costa Rica. "You take people up, they have an experience, they see things, it impacts them viscerally, and intellectually, and so maybe they land and it changes their life," explained Matthew Hess, LightHawk's director. "Maybe they vote differently on the next bill."[8]

They will float wacky conspiracy theories to control property. In his book, *The War Against the Greens* (Sierra Club Books), David Helvarg explains that the Moonies are the ones trying to rewrite

---

8. *The New York Times*, 18 March 1996.

American environmental laws. His evidence? "A Japanese-owned pulpmill in Sitka, Alaska had been the main beneficiary of below-cost logging in the Tongass National Forest until late 1993 . . . Also, the Mitsubishi corporation has been the main purchaser of raw logs from Weyerhauser, which now finds itself losing market share to finished paper products from Japan. The Japanese are also grazing beef cattle on public lands in Montana and are the main purchasers of Alaskan fish, including haddock and other species facing commercial extinction owing to overharvesting." The fact that Rev. Sun Myung Moon is Korean, and that Koreans retain a deep resentment against the Japanese because of its colonial period, is apparently lost on Helvarg. Does Sierra Club Books want to bring back "the yellow peril?"

No one should be surprised that there is a double standard when it comes to reporting extremism on the right and the left. Talk radio is lambasted as extreme, but how many newspaper articles have you read blaming environmental groups for creating "a climate of hate" and making the Unabomber possible? When the National Rifle Association and radio talk show host G. Gordon Liddy referred to some federal law enforcement officials as "thugs," the media outcry was deafening. But nary a peep is heard when the Sierra Club names yours truly "Eco-Thug of the Month" in a publication *Sierra Magazine,* sent to 550,000 subscribers.

"The mainstream environmental groups are quickly becoming irrelevant," wrote Mike Roselle in *Earth First! Journal.* "What we want is nothing short of a revolution. . . . F— that crap you read in 'Wild Earth' or in 'Confessions of an Eco-Warrior.' Monkeywrenching is more than just sabotage, and you're goddam right, it's revolutionary. This is *jihad,* pal. There are no innocent bystanders, because in these desperate hours, bystanders are not innocent." You have been buried with details about right-wing militia groups. How many of you heard about the animal welfare group that was stockpiling assault weapons in Los Angeles? Mercy Crusade Inc. bought the guns for its twelve humane officers, who have *arrest powers in animal abuse cases* under an eighty-year-old state law. The group had over $100,000 in weaponry. Have you read about the Environmental Rangers, who wear sidearms and patrol the Blackfoot River region in Montana? Their leader, Ric Valois has pledged to wage "a war, and I mean a real war" to stop a local mining operation. How did the *Los Angeles Times* report on this group? It said: "Conservationists have seen traditional avenues of protest diminish. A Republican majority has closed many options on the legislative front."[9] Funny, the Branch Davidians weren't excused because a Democratic majority passed gun control laws.

But, on the issue of private property, the eco-federal coalition owes more to communism than to any other philosophy. You don't have to read very far into environmentalists' writings to find its statist slant. The thread runs from the far left (biologist Barry Commoner believes it is time to consider the "faults of the U.S. capitalist system from the vantage point of a socialist alternative") to the center left (Vice President Al Gore complaining of the "shortcomings of capitalist economics as it is now practiced."). When former Soviet President Mikhail Gorbachev found himself forced from communism (and then from power), his instincts took him immediately to embrace environmentalism. Today the Gorbachev Foundation is prestigious, despite the history of the man who presided over Chernobyl and the subsequent cover-up of the disaster.

Carl Bloice is a writer/editor who belonged to the Communist Party USA until the party fractured over the coup in the Soviet Union and the subsequent collapse of the Evil Empire. "The environmental movement promises to bring greater numbers into our orbit than the peace movement ever did," he wrote in March 1995.

"With the collapse of Communism—particularly of socialist economic theory—environmentalism has become freedom's foe for

---

9. *National Review West*, 26 February 1996.

the '90s," wrote Robert Bidinotto, staff writer for *Reader's Digest*. "Environmentalism represents a now-denuded Marxism, stripped of all its tenets, desperately clutching its last fig leaf of mindless egalitarianism. As such, it is a purely negative, contentless 'ism.' It is the final rallying point for nihilistic drifters and collectivist dreamers, who are united, not by ideas, but by a hostility toward human thought; not by values, but by an aversion for human aspirations; not by some utopian vision of society, but by a profound alienation from human society."

Unlike the Bolsheviks, who crushed or co-opted their enemies to hold on to power for over seventy years, the eco-federal coalition has broad-based opposition that is growing in strength. Some are single-issue groups, some are more generalized. Some fight against regulations at the local level, others in the courts, and others use the Constitution. It is a movement with no leader, but hundreds of thousands of active supporters. Its banner reads: "Don't Tread on Me!" Its cause is property rights.

9

THE PROPERTY RIGHTS MOVEMENT

*"We're going to take on these phony property rights advocates
and kick their butts."*

—DEBBIE SEASE OF THE SIERRA CLUB

Asked if big corporations were backing him, Chuck Cushman of the American Land Rights Association said: "I wish they were. Our whole budget is $300,000 a year."

For years, environmentalists have been ridiculing fledgling property rights groups as the creatures of corporate interests. In fact, the largest of these organizations cannot compete financially with the smallest national environmental groups. There is no cash cow to be milked in the property rights movement. There is no "Property Rights Grantmakers Association." What corporate donations they get are from local companies trying to stay in business. People like

Chuck Cushman never get invited to visit the Rockefeller Foundation.

Cushman is one of the "Founding Fathers" of the property rights movement. The American Land Rights Association (ALRA) used to be the National Inholders Association. Inholders are landowners whose property is surrounded or restricted by federal land, usually national parks or wildlife refuges. Unlike the big green groups, ALRA isn't headquartered in Washington, DC. It is appropriately located in Battle Ground, Washington. And unlike these same green groups, ALRA receives no taxpayer money. The group's fax network connects it with hundreds of other property rights organizations in an effort to get their concerns aired in Washington and in state legislatures across the country. Cushman knows why there is a property rights movement. "As the environmentalists dig deeper and go for the throat on private property, especially wetlands and endangered species, at some point a critical mass would be achieved."

PEGGY REIGLE

Peggy Reigle had retired from her job at the *New York Daily News* and moved with her husband to Cambridge, Maryland. A neighbor asked her for help because of trouble with wetlands regulations. When she saw what was common practice for the U.S. Army Corps of Engineers, she established the Fairness to Land Owners Committee (FLOC). "Under the guise of saving the environment, the opposition is fleecing landowners of their right to the prudent use and enjoyment of their land," she declares. "Legislators, bureaucrats and environmental hucksters are waging war against the *real* environmentalists—those who own and tend the land; those who produce the food and fiber for this great Nation."

Reigle says that 90 percent of the property rights abuses she sees concern the corps's wetlands policies. "These predators are stripping senior citizens of their retirement nest eggs," she explains. "They are killing the American Dream of affordable housing for the young and the less affluent. They are trampling on constitutionally guaranteed private property rights. And they are destroying our economy." Reigle also knows from where the strength of the movement comes: "Unlike industry groups that fear the power of the greens and—hoping to ward off attacks—give enormous contributions to the environmental community, landowners are not about to give up their land and their Constitutional rights to the folly of the 'green giants.'" In five years, The FLOC has grown to 15,000 member landowners in fifty states. The FLOC receives no tax money.

JEFF HARRIS

Jeff Harris runs People for the West! in Pueblo, Colorado. "People out here really came to believe that the traditional Western way of life was coming under assault. Our growth, I think, has been a natural response." His director of operations, Guy Baier, also knows where the strength of the property rights movement lies: "The great majority of our membership are the small-scale resource producers. We like to say they're the ones with mud on their boots." People for the West! has 15,000 members in 121 chapters from Burro Creek, Arizona, to Battle Mountain, Nevada. People for the West! receives no tax money.

NANCIE AND ROGER MARZULLA

Nancie and Roger Marzulla are the organizers of Defenders of Property Rights in Washington, DC. They believe that property rights is going to become the civil rights issue of the 1990s. Nancie's editorials have been published in major newspapers across the country. "When we started out, nobody really took the issue seriously," she recalls. "But government intrusion and regulations have become so severe and widespread that property rights has become a real force." Nancie Marzulla knows who the Defenders of Property Rights are. "This issue involves a broad cross-section of Americans—this is not an industry platform," she remarks. "What we have been showing is that it is truly a broad, grassroots movement that has caught fire and that it is not going to go away." Defenders of Property Rights has an annual budget of $250,000 a year and receives no tax money. Big Business money cannot be found anywhere near Defenders of Property Rights. "The only corporation that sent us a check is Mobile Oil," explains Nancie, "and they sent us a check for $25."

And there are many, many more people heading organizations to give beleaguered property owners a fighting chance: William Perry Pendley and the Mountain States Legal Foundation of Denver, Colorado; Ron Arnold's Center for the Defense of Free Enterprise in Bellevue, Washington; Bruce Vincent's Alliance for America in Caroga Lake, New York; Judy Cresanta and the Nevada Policy Research Institute in Reno, Nevada; Terry L. Anderson and his associates with the Political Economy Research Center (PERC) in Bozeman, Montana; Robert K. Best of the Pacific Legal Foundation; and John Carlson of the Washington Institute for Policy Studies in Seattle, Washington.

This is just a small sampling of the number of true grassroots organizations that have sprung up in response to the depredations of the eco-federal coalition. The phenomenon is not restricted to the western United States. There is the Property Rights Foundation of America in Stony Creek, New York. This group so disturbed the National Audubon Society it sent out a press release saying, "If you thought the wise use and private property rights movements were only prevalent in the western United States, think again. This movement may be alive and well here in New York State if the Property Rights Foundation of America (PRFA) has its way." It is very important for people not to dismiss property rights as a western regional issue. "One of the main things we're trying to do here is translate the issue and bring it to the attention of people in urban areas," says Donald Schmitz of the Fifth Amendment Foundation. "We need to communicate in suburban and urban areas a very important issue here: that you can be secure in your possessions without the government taking them away from you. . . . We are people who reject the notion that individual liberties can be trampled on for the greater good."

There may be as many as 2,000 property rights organizations in the United States. They blanket the nation from coast to coast and across great distances to Alaska and Hawaii. From the Alaska Wetlands Coalition to the Hawaii Island Geothermal Alliance to California Women in Timber to Arizonans for Private Property Rights to the Wyoming Resource Providers Coalition to the Private Landowners of Wisconsin to the Vermont Property Rights Center to the Maine Conservation Rights Institute, these organizations provide encouragement and legal support to people like the Clines and the Hecks and the Millses—people who have lost money or freedom in fights with the government over endangered species or wetlands.

TRUE GRASSROOTS

These groups are not the tools of corporations, and the environmentalists know it. "We have come to the conclusion that this is pretty much generally a grass-roots movement," Debra Callahan, director of the W. Alton Jones Foundation's Environmental Grass Roots Program, said in a closed door meeting of environmentalists worried about the property rights movement. "[This] is a problem," she continued, "because it means there's no silver bullet." Moreover, she added, "this is happening in every single state. We think of this as being a western phenomenon—it's not true."[1] When Greenpeace compiled a list of over fifty "anti-environmental organizations," including many property rights groups, their combined annual budgets were still less than Greenpeace's budget alone.

When environmentalists do uncover an organization that is supported by mining or oil interests, they trumpet it to a gullible media. The Audubon Society thought it had achieved a coup when it revealed that the Western Public Lands Coalition received 96 percent of its $1.7 million budget from corporate donors. But compared to the Audubon Society itself, this is chump change. Audubon's budget is $37.3 million. More than $10 million of that comes from grants by corporate foundations. It receives more than $1.1 million from its *own royalties and mineral rights* from natural gas wells it operates on the Rainey Wildlife Sanctuary in Louisiana. It spends more than *four times* the entire annual budget of the Western Public Lands Coalition on fund-raising and administration alone.

When U.S. senators and representatives began speaking up for property rights on the floor of Congress, the caterwauling from the eco-federal coalition could be heard across the Potomac. The efforts of Representative Don Young (R-Arkansas), Representative Helen Chenoweth (R-Idaho), Senator Frank Murkowski (R-Arkansas), Senator Ted Stevens (R-Arkansas), Representative Jim Hansen (R-Utah), Senator Conrad Burns (R-Montana), and myself prompted Richard Lacayo of *Time* magazine to write a piece entitled "This Land Is Whose Land?" in which he informed his readers "From out of the West comes a strike force of Congressmen and Senators who think natural resources ought to be exploited, not coddled." Yes, we

---

1. *Trashing the Economy*, pp. 42–43.

were labeled the tools of corporate interests as well.

"Today environmental policy is not about safety, or survivability, or sustainability, but about achieving power and control over people's lives," says William Perry Pendley, author of *War on the West*. He is correct. In Congress, we see the effect of government at work every day. Most of us are well aware that a single sentence or word in a piece of legislation will have far-reaching effects on the citizens of the United States. Such power makes congressional supporters of property rights cautious and mindful of legislation's effects. Unfortunately, it creates an insatiable appetite for control over other people's property in others. The battle cannot be won on Capitol Hill alone. Even well-intentioned legislation can be twisted by the bureaucracy. "Many of the worst stories of government abuse come not so much from the laws themselves but from the bureaucratic attitudes of the enforcers that the government lets loose on the rest of us," writes Robert K. Best of the Pacific Legal Foundation. "Unelected bureaucrats separate themselves from you and me and the real world we live in. Their priorities are their jobs, their power and their prestige. As a result, too many drop all sense of reason and pursue regulation as an end in itself."[2]

The battle over private property rights is more than just a political struggle. Policymakers who fail to realize this are doomed to be ignored and rejected. The eco-federal coalition intimidates moderates of both parties by citing polls that show widespread public support for environmental protection. But when these surveys ask people about compensation for takings or endangered species restrictions, the numbers swing the other way. President Clinton and his Secretary of the Interior, Bruce Babbitt, are certainly prime examples of politicians who have little grasp of the problem. While proposing and enforcing policies that undermine property rights,

---

2. *In Perspective*, Summer 1995, p. 3.

they also find themselves under fire from their allies in the environmental movement who think the pace of property seizure should be stepped up. "There is a good chance that he [Clinton] has lost control of the agenda," said Jon Roush, president of the Wilderness Society. "The people who oppose him are people who want it all, and they are accustomed to getting it all."[3]

That quote, coming from Mr. Roush, is highly ironic, as you will see in the next chapter. The people who "want it all" are the leaders of the environmental movement, and they are willing to go to any lengths to get "it." Opposing them are people with a little bit of land who cannot afford to hire high-powered attorneys or Washington lobbyists. These landowners often cannot compete on Capitol Hill. But on their home ground, they are tenacious. Let us remove ourselves from the rear echelons and see what is happening on the front lines of the green war.

---

3. "Clinton: How the West Was Lost," by Claude R. Marx, *Investor's Business Daily*, 1 September 1994, p. 1

10

ON THE FRONTIERS
OF THE GREEN WAR

"If wolves leave the park and kill livestock, that would just be a risk the rancher would have to take."

—A SUPPORTER OF THE REINTRODUCTION OF THE GRAY WOLF
INTO YELLOWSTONE NATIONAL PARK

It was overcast and gray in Salmon, Idaho, on Sunday, 22 January 1995. The temperature was 20 degrees with a chilly breeze. It was not the kind of day you would want to spend standing around outside. Early in the afternoon, cars, trucks, tractors, and other farm vehicles began to appear at the Lemhi County fairgrounds. By two o'clock the grandstands were full, and the string of vehicles stretched for miles. Parents protected their infants from the cold and old-timers were supported by neighbors. They were over 2,500 local people at the fairgrounds from two towns with a total population of 4,000 . . . to get their picture taken.

They posed for that photograph to show U.S. District Court Judge David Alan Ezra of Hawaii who they were. Judge Ezra (substituting for a federal judge in Idaho who was ill) had just issued an injunction against all mining, timber, grazing, firewood gathering, and road building activities on federal land in six Idaho forests. Unfortunately for the citizens of Salmon, Challis, and surrounding communities, 93 percent of Lemhi County (population 7,000) is federally owned. The injunction affected 14 million acres of Idaho's most productive land. The shutdown of industry in the forests would lead to a loss of almost 19,000 jobs in the state. "We all sat around and read it, and we just couldn't believe it," said Donna Brady, a Challis resident whose husband works for Hecla Grouse Creek Gold Mine. She said most mining families could not last even a few months without income.

The injunction was ordered as a result of a lawsuit by the Pacific Rivers Council, Sierra Club Legal Defense Fund and the Wilderness Society. These environmental organizations claimed that the U.S. Forest Service had not consulted with the National Marine Fisheries Service when it drafted its long-range forest management plan. They claimed to be out to protect the winter run of the endangered Chinook salmon. Because of the Forest Service's failure to follow procedure, the lawsuit called for the banning of all logging, grazing, mining, and road building activities—even those the Forest Service had determined were "not likely to adversely affect" the salmon. Judge Ezra ruled that the injunction would remain in effect until all questions of Forest Service compliance with the Endangered Species Act had been resolved. Thousands of Idahoans were to be left jobless because agencies of the federal government failed to get their work done on time.

Judge Ezra was unconcerned with the fact that the citizens of Salmon would be out of work while the Forest Service went through the process of complying with the court order. The plaintiffs certainly did not care about the endangered livelihoods in Lemhi County. "This is a victory for Idaho's salmon," said Kristen Boyles, an attorney for the Sierra Club Legal Defense Fund. "There is a misperception that protecting salmon habitat pits the environment against jobs," explained Bob Doppelt, executive director of The Pacific Rivers Council, "but, in fact, the issue is jobs versus jobs—a few jobs today versus many more jobs tomorrow and in the future."[1]

The University of Idaho produced a study to determine what effect the injunction would have on surrounding communities. The results were grim. Over $43 million in earnings and an immediate loss of 1,400 jobs would occur in these tiny towns. "It appears fair to say," the report concluded, "that since the economies of Custer and Lemhi Counties are so dependent on the use of renewable and non-renewable natural resources that this injunction, if implemented, will decimate them. In the very short term, they are facing a loss of 40 percent of earnings (wages plus proprietors' disposable income) and 29 percent of full-time jobs."

The injunction would not cost any jobs at the Pacific Rivers Council. No jobs would be lost at the Sierra Club Legal Defense Fund or Wilderness Society. Nor would any jobs be lost at the U.S. Forest Service or the National Marine Fisheries Service, the people responsible for the coordination problem. Only the miners, farmers, mill workers, and people whose livelihoods depended on their business would lose jobs. Those theoretical "many jobs" in the future wouldn't pay the mortgage. The Pacific Rivers Council didn't care about that. "Public outcry and doomsday predictions are to be expected when people feel blind-sided," said Doppelt, "and when the binge of overuse is forced to an end."[2]

One would think six national forests would be enough for the Chinook salmon. Not so, said the Pacific Rivers Council: "New watershed protection and restoration policies must extend beyond the Upper Columbia basin to include *all* federal lands in the northern Rockies, including those east of the continental divide." Why? To

---

1. Letter from Doppelt to President Clinton dated 1 February 1995.
2. Ibid.

protect the Chinook salmon, steelhead, bull trout, rainbow trout, white sturgeon, river-dwelling Arctic grayling, shiny headed sculpin, Idaho giant salamanders, boreal toads, Pacific chorus frogs, tailed frogs, spotted frogs, river mussels, and rare plants and aquatic species.

LOCAL RESPONSE

There are many groups in Idaho interested in preserving the salmon. Interestingly, none of them agreed with the injunction. "The Commission wishes the environmentalists who filed this disruptive lawsuit would join our staff in solving problems rather than further polarizing this complex issue with legal actions," said Jerry Conley, director of the Idaho Fish and Game Commission.

"This injunction will do little good for Idaho's salmon and steelhead while causing pain and harm to many Idahoans who also want these fish restored," said Mitch Sanchutena, executive coordinator of Idaho Steelhead and Salmon Unlimited.

"There's no way this is going to help make the salmon come back," said Jack Cook. Cook is a local citizen in his eighties with a scrapbook full of thirty years of clippings, describing his efforts to save the salmon. "It makes me feel like an innocent person is being sent to the gallows."

The court injunction was curiously limited if its purpose was to protect the salmon. Mining, logging, and grazing were banned, but not recreation, river rafting, wildlife management, firefighting, hatcheries, and ski resorts—all of which can also compromise the integrity of the salmon's natural habitat.

"This ruling is good for Idaho's environment and Idaho's economy. Clean water and healthy fish are far more important to Idaho than 19th century resource extraction industries," said Craig Gehrke, director of Wilderness Society's Boise office.

Gehrke probably uses a computer, which cannot be manufactured without those "19th century resource extraction industries." If he owns a home, it contains hundreds of thousands of pounds of minerals extracted by mining. Materials to build the mountain bikes and fishing rods that naturalists so love had to be mined. In fact, if Gehrke and his friends at the Wilderness Society are average, they each utilize twenty tons of new minerals annually.

MEANWHILE, IN FLORENCE . . .

While Gehrke spoke, and the citizens of Salmon gathered together for their photo, loggers were hard at work cutting down trees in the Bitterroot Valley—a mere 100 miles north of Salmon, near the town of Florence in western Montana. A wealthy local landowner with a 736-acre, $2.5 million ranch wanted to clear eighty acres of old-growth Douglas fir and ponderosa pine from his land. The area being cut was less than two miles from the boundary of the Bitterroot National Forest and well within the so-called Salmon/Selway Ecosystem. Nearby Sweeney Creek is home to the bull trout—under consideration to be designated a threatened species because of, environmentalists claim, increased sedimentation due to logging and road building required to reach suitable trees.

In 1983, the U.S. Forest Service wanted to cut trees in the Bitterroot Forest but was stopped by a Wilderness Society lawsuit. The environmental organization claimed that logging could be disastrous to the rivers, streams, and wildlife in the area. The suit severely restricted Forest Service logging—limiting it to 66,700 board feet of timber in the past three years. This new private timber cut was six times greater—over 400,000 board feet—worth at least $140,000 to the owner.

This landowner was not concerned. He cut down the older, more valuable trees. He left only a 100-foot buffer strip of trees next to the stream instead of the 300-foot buffer advocated by the Wilderness Society. He collected the bounty of his harvested trees—an amount of money only slightly more than his annual salary of $125,000. This landowner was G. Jon Roush, Craig Gehrke's boss and president of the Wilderness Society.

Roush took over the organization in January 1994 after working his way up through the environmental movement, serving as the executive vice president of The Nature Conservancy before taking over at the Wilderness Society. The Society has 300,000 members and an annual budget of $16 million. Jean Hocker, president of the Land Trust Alliance, described Roush as someone "with a real feel for the land." Evidently.

Alexander Cockburn and Jeffrey St. Clair of the leftist publication *The Nation* uncovered Roush's timber sale and had this to say about it: "The head of the Wilderness Society logging old growth in the Bitterroot Valley is roughly akin to the head of Human Rights Watch torturing a domestic servant."

Roush had his excuses all ready. The logging was designed to "improve the ecological conditions." The area was "overstocked" and needed to be "thinned." The sale was "better managed" and "more environmentally conscious" than any other. His property was "not particularly sensitive" ecologically. He needed the money as part of a separation settlement with his wife.

Roush found unexpected allies in the property rights movement. Chuck Cushman of the American Land Rights Association congratulated Roush for his "so-far eloquent defense of private property rights." The Montana Wood Products Association offered to hold an Honor Roush Day.

Roush had signed a Wilderness Society fund-raising letter scolding timber companies that "measure the value of land only in dollars, in board-feet of lumber." But when he needed the money, he exercised the rights he had fought all his life to deny to other property owners—he used the land to benefit himself and his family.

G. Jon Roush, a former professor of English literature at Reed College in Portland, Oregon, is a proletarian compared to most members of the environmental leadership. His predecessor as head of the Wilderness Society, George T. Frampton Jr. is more typical. Frampton graduated from Yale, got his master's degree from the London School of Economics, and his J.D. from Harvard Law School. He served as a law clerk to U.S. Supreme Court Justice Harry A. Blackmun, and as a special prosecutor on the Watergate Special Prosecution Force. He then established his own law practice before taking over The Wilderness Society in 1986. He left in 1993 to become Assistant Secretary of the Interior for Fish and Wildlife.

Average Americans like those of Salmon, Idaho, have no way to match the connections of Roush and Frampton. The citizens of Lemhi County, locked in battle with the "green giants"—the large environmental organizations—could hardly fend off the raw power of the federal government and its agencies. While the court fight to keep the national forests open went on, and while Roush chopped down his trees nearby, the U.S. Government, through its Fish and Wildlife Service, had opened yet another front in Lemhi County.

GRAY WOLVES

In 1991, Congress directed the U.S. Fish and Wildlife Service to prepare a draft environmental impact statement on the reintroduction of gray wolves into Yellowstone National Park and central Idaho. "Our goal must be to preserve every kind of weed and fly the earth is now blessed with, except a very few that present a known health threat," said Arthur Unger of the Sierra Club. "Once a species is extinct, it cannot be brought back to life. We do know that we can extinguish any population, but those who come centuries after us may not be able to create higher life forms." Mr. Unger does not believe that the wolf—which kills far more than it can eat—can be considered "a known health threat."

The Endangered Species Act does not mandate the reintroduction of wolves. This was an effort that was undertaken by the Fish and Wildlife Service voluntarily. In fact, there is scanty evidence that there ever were wolves in the Yellowstone area. The records of early scouts like Jim Bridger do not mention wolves. The government, however, was on a mission. The effect of wolf packs on human communities and associated livestock was glossed over. The environmental impact statement for central Idaho declared that placing wolves into the area would have no impact on private property. Coupled with the avid support of wildlife groups, who submitted petitions with 89,000 signatures supporting reintroduction of the wolves, the government's case was made. Local ranchers could not complete with this onslaught, despite the fact that they were the ones who would have to live with the decision. "Very few people visiting Yellowstone Park would ever get to see a free-roaming wolf," said one rancher, "while landowners and ranchers would be continually subjected to livestock losses and harassment by wolves."

One petitioner illustrated the environmentalists' feelings about this line of reasoning: "If wolves leave the park and kill livestock, that would just be a risk the rancher would have to take."

"I am personally very tired of hearing from ranchers in regard to their livestock," complained another reintroduction supporter. "I feel the animals of the wild should be completely protected and livestock should go! By putting livestock and ranchers first, we are putting nature in a terrible, unbalanced situation. . . ."

"There were wolves in the New York City area at one time," replied one rancher. "Why not plant a few there?" The analogy was appropriate, according to Idaho Attorney General Alan G. Lance. He said, "If U.S. Fish and Wildlife thought it would be a good idea to reintroduce bison to the traditional ranges of bison within the

Great Plains, and thereby impact upon agriculture and economic activity in Chicago and Indiana and the farming operations there, what outcry would we hear from the constituents of that State or those States?"[3]

Ultimately, Fish and Wildlife Service officials adopted a plan to reintroduce the wolves (at a cost of $7 million plus $334,000 to track them for five years). They did come up with what they felt was an acceptable compromise. The wolves would be reintroduced, but local landowners would be permitted to kill a wolf if he caught it in the act of threatening his family or livestock on his land. On January 14, eight days before the photo at the Lemhi County fairgrounds, the first four gray wolves were released in Lemhi County. They had been flown in from Alberta, Canada. On January 20 one particular young female wolf, numbered B13, was set free at the Indian Creek landing strip, about sixty miles from Salmon.

At eleven o'clock on the morning of January 29, Eugene Hussey and his workers went outside to check on his cows. The seventy-five-year-old rancher owns 400 head of cattle on an area of ten miles by fifteen miles near Iron Creek, adjoining Highway 93 between the towns of Salmon and Challis. His father had bought the land in 1916. Hussey's land includes some forest, so he was facing a possible end to the lifestyle handed down from his father because of the court injunction.

As he approached the cows, Hussey spotted something. "We looked down from a ridge and saw the calf in the brush with what looked like a dog on the ground beside it," he said. When he got closer he saw that the "dog" had a Fish and Wildlife Service collar and a green tag with the number 13 on it. The animal had been shot through the chest. The remains of a half-eaten calf lay next to it.

---

3. Testimony before House Subcommittee on Resource Conservation, Research, and Forestry and House subcommittee on Fisheries, Wildlife, and Oceans. 104th Congress, 1st Session. 30 March 1995.

Hussey's cows had often been victimized by coyotes and he had given permission to hunters to shoot any coyote they saw in that pasture. He thought the shooter may have mistaken wolf B13 for a coyote.

Hussey headed back to the house and called the Idaho Cattle Association to find out what to do. A board member told him to report the death, but in the meantime to gather his own evidence. Hussey called Dr. Robert Cope, his regular veterinarian, and asked him to perform an autopsy on the calf and the wolf. Dr. Cope told Hussey that the calf had been born live and had been on its feet before it died. He found mother's milk in the calf. He found meat from the calf in the wolf's stomach. Later studies showed the wolf had eaten from two other cows and a deer in the less than nine days it had been free in Idaho.

Hussey then called Brett Barsalou, the Lemhi County sheriff, and the Fish and Wildlife Service. FWS officials told Hussey he was not a "suspect" in the shooting. "Evidence strongly suggests that the wolf picked up the calf, carried it about 100 to 150 yards, put it down and maybe took a couple of bites," said Ted Koch of the Fish and Wildlife Service. "We aren't sure yet whether or not the wolf killed the calf, but circumstantial evidence is pretty strong."

Wolf B13 was frozen and transported to the Ashland Forensics Laboratory in Oregon. Since neither Hussey nor his workers shot the wolf, it was an illegal act. The lab soon claimed that their autopsies on the wolf and the calf "indicate that the dead wolf did not kill the calf," and that the calf "is believed to have been stillborn or to have died from natural causes shortly after birth." The Fish and Wildlife Service actually ordered DNA testing of the contents of the wolf's stomach.

Dr. Cope reported that the calf could not have been stillborn as its lungs were inflated. He said the calf appeared to have died from multiple lacerations inflicted by the wolf.

The death of wolf B13 received national media attention. The

Fish and Wildlife Service released a press statement saying an autopsy had been conducted by the University of Oregon School of Veterinary Medicine. The problem is that the University of Oregon has no school of veterinary medicine. On the *ABC Evening News,* Peter Jennings reported that a rancher had shot the wolf. No such determination had been made. Jennings also neglected to mention the presence of the dead calf.

Hussey began to receive threats. One telephone caller said, "We are going to come up there and kill cows, in order to pay for the wolf." Sheriff Barsalou soon began to receive hate mail from around the country. A woman from Texas accused the sheriff of covering up the circumstances of the shooting. "I hope you and your sheriffs have the guts enough to be fair and truly investigate this slaughter," she wrote. "If you don't, then all of you Idahoans are a bunch of trigger-happy, land-hogging bureaucrats."

Another woman, this one from Arizona, asked Sheriff Barsalou if he was proud of his "redneck ranchers up there." She called Hussey "a murderer, plain and simple" and told the sheriff "if you can't get your trigger-happy bozos under control, I might be convinced of the efficacy of setting leg traps in the parking lot of your local Dunkin' Donuts."

On March 8, almost six weeks later, three armed agents of the U.S. Fish and Wildlife Service arrived on Hussey's property with a search warrant, claiming to be looking for the fatal bullet. This was curious in itself. Even if they had found the expended bullet, it would have had very little evidentiary value without the firearm it came from.

"As I got there," said Hussey, "Feds were crawling over my gate. They had broke one wire. And I said, 'Get your butts back,' I said, 'You're not coming on this property until the sheriff gets here.' " The three agents walked along the south side of the creek while Hussey paralleled their movements on the north side. He was unarmed, but he did pick up two softball-size rocks. When Hussey asked why he hadn't been notified that the agents were coming, one replied, "Oh, you subsidized farmers," Hussey later explained, "We won't talk about what I said then because I don't know what in the hell I said because I just go off my gourd."

Another agent said to Hussey, "Well, if you don't like this country, why don't you go to another?" At this point, Sheriff Barsalou, summoned by one of Hussey's workers, arrived at the scene. "Their [the agents'] guns were visible to me when I walked up," said Barsalou. "When I walked up, there were three grown, trained law enforcement officers standing around a seventy-five-year-old man in a screaming match. That's what I saw." Hussey told Barsalou that the agents had touched their gun holsters during the confrontation.

The sheriff tried to calm the situation, but he felt the wildlife officers' treatment of both himself and Hussey "was inappropriate, heavy-handed and dangerously close to excessive force," according to the twenty-three-year law enforcement officer. "I asked them specifically if Mr. Hussey got in their way if they were going to arrest him, and they wouldn't answer that question. They just said they were going to search. I then said, 'Well, you know, three to one is not really fair odds. If you do decide to arrest Mr. Hussey, are you going to arrest me if I come to his assistance?' And they said yes, that's what they were going to do. The supervisor said, 'If it's necessary.' "

Barsalou went over to Hussey and said, "Gene, let's get out of here. They've got more guns than we have." The agents subsequently left Hussey's property, their "search" incomplete.

U.S. Department of Justice officials were soon suggesting that both Mr. Hussey and the sheriff were "obstructing justice." The brouhaha brought in local and state authorities, as well as Idaho's congressional representatives and senators.

On March 10, Representative Helen Chenoweth, Representative Michael Crapo, Senator Larry Craig, and Senator Dirk Kempthorne met with Mollie Beattie, director of the U.S. Fish and

Wildlife Service. She admitted that her agents made mistakes serving the search warrant on Hussey. Beattie "did not deny claims by Lemhi County commissioners and Sheriff Brett Barsalou that the rancher, Mr. Hussey, may have been intimidated and that Barsalou was not consulted." Beattie said that her people should have been more cooperative with local law enforcement agents.

The Idaho representatives were not satisfied. "The Fish and Wildlife Service must answer with regard to a number of issues," said Representative Crapo. "What evidence exists that a crime has been committed? What grounds were used to justify obtaining a search warrant? What is Fish and Wildlife policy regarding the proper relationship with state and local government in the conduct of enforcement actions and investigations?"

On March 30, a joint hearing of congressional subcommittees was held on Capitol Hill. Sheriff Barsalou, Mr. Hussey, Attorney General Lance, and Mark Pollot, director of the Constitutional Law Center for the Stewards of the Range, were there to testify. Pollot raised a startling contention early in the proceedings: "Assuming constitutional authority exists for the United States to authorize Fish and Wildlife Service employees to carry weapons, arrest suspected offenders, and to undertake other police actions, an examination of the statute establishing and governing the Service demonstrates that Congress did not delegate such authority to the Service. . . . Congress did not intend the Service to have a police force all of its own . . . they were not authorized by this Act to undertake such actions and those actions were unlawful."

Even if we assume Pollot is wrong, we can still ask whether these Fish and Wildlife Service agents were best suited for the job at hand—which was serving a search warrant and finding a spent bullet. Wouldn't violation of federal law require the presence of the FBI?

If Fish and Wildlife Service agents carrying automatic weapons does not disturb you, how about agents of the National Marine Fisheries Service? Dr. Greg Matlock, program management officer testified to the joint committee: "In this regard, our Enforcement Office acts as the multi-agency coordinator of strategic and tactical enforcement efforts undertaken by the [Columbia Basin Law Enforcement] council. Perhaps the most visible program developed under the council in gravel-to-gravel protection is the salmon enforcement team. . . . Since salmon travel widely during their life cycle, it makes good sense to place officers where and when they are most needed. When adult salmon reach Idaho to spawn, the Idaho State Department of Fish and Game asks the other salmon enforcement team agencies to send officers to help." (To help enforcement, I assume, not to help spawn.)

Mollie Beattie, director of the Fish and Wildlife Service, also testified. She made the astounding assertion that the agents on Hussey's land did not even require a search warrant under the open fields doctrine of the Supreme Court. When Representative Chenoweth challenged her on this—reminding her that the open fields doctrine applied only to evidence that was in plain sight—Beattie backtracked. She also stated for the record, "I have nothing but praise of the actions of these agents."

Hussey related his story to the panel and reminded them that he served in World War II and received the Silver Star. "I like to be treated like an American," Hussey told the panel. He has since filed a lawsuit against the U.S. Government. He wants $500 to replace the loss of his calf.

"If these same type of agents with the same attitude return to central Idaho counties," warned Sheriff Barsalou, "they will not only have problems with the citizens they work for, but if they try it in my country, they'll definitely have problems with me."

"I can't get past this point in my own mind that a live, healthy citizen is more important than a dead wolf," said Barsalou. The sheriff is apparently unqualified for a position with the Fish and Wildlife Service.

Despite the declarations of their director, as to their sensitivity to the rights of humans, Fish and Wildlife Service agents continued their single-minded pursuit of the heinous criminal. This notice appeared in Idaho newspapers:

REWARD

Reward up to $5000 for information leading to the conviction of the person or persons responsible for the unlawful killing of wolves in Idaho.

On April 26, one of the wolves released in Yellowstone National Park went missing. Biologists found the wolf's radio collar but not the wolf. Suspecting foul play, Fish and Wildlife agents again went into action. Within *days* they arrested Chad McKittrick, an unemployed carpenter, from Red Lodge, Montana. McKittrick thought he was shooting a dog or a coyote. "I didn't know it was a wolf," he told federal agents. His hunting companion claimed McKittrick *did* know it was a wolf. Agents found the wolf's head and hide at McKittrick's house.

McKittrick was charged with a misdemeanor, which brings a maximum sentence of a year in prison and a $50,000 fine. He was ultimately convicted and sentenced to six months in prison and a $10,000 fine. Now local residents are worried. "People want to make Montana a playground," said Averill Keller, who raises cattle and sheep in the area. "But some of us have to make a living here. More and more, our private property rights are being taken away from us." The FWS wolf recovery coordinator for Montana suggested that the ranchers drop their objections, reasoning that the quicker the wolf population grows, the sooner they will be taken off the endangered species list. Montana state representative Alvin Ellis found this logic a little hard to swallow. "It's a little like saying that you can't control cockroaches or rats until there are so many in any given city. It's absurd!" he said.

Senator Conrad Burns of Montana had a different view of the matter. He introduced legislation to cut off funding for the wolf reintroduction. "They ain't gonna get no more," he vowed in his usual eloquent style. His bill reduced funding for the reintroduction program to $100,000 for Fiscal Year 1995.

THE FORGOTTEN FRONTIER

Most people have never heard the story of Lemhi County or Red Lodge, Montana. They do not know about the photo of Salmon residents or G. Jon Roush's timber harvest or Eugene Hussey's harassment. Places like Lemhi County are "flyover country"—far from the centers of news and culture. When I held hearings as the head of the House Endangered Species Act Reform Task Force, I was severely criticized for setting them up in rural areas or smaller cities— places like Belle Chasse, Louisiana; New Bern, North Carolina; Boerne, Texas; and Bakersfield, California—not in major urban areas, where environmentalists say the law is supported. But that was just the point. In the middle of New York City, they do not have a big endangered species problem. I wanted to hear from the individuals who have been affected by federal environmental regulation, not paid lobbyists from some air-conditioned office in the midst of a city of eight million people.

Leroy Ornellas, a third-generation dairy farmer from Tracy, California, summed up the need for reform of the Endangered Species Act (ESA) this way:

"Several hundred years ago you owned property at the whim of monarchs. If you displeased the King or Emperor, he would send in his army, confiscate your property, have you beheaded, give your property to one of his favorite subjects who, in turn, would probably marry your widow. This type of tyranny does not exist in this country today. In its place, we have a more subtle form of tyranny. It is called the ESA."

Eco-leaders are used to winning their fights with like-minded judges in the courtrooms and with like-minded bureaucrats in Washington, DC. Their victims, however, are everywhere. They are the ranchers, farmers, miners, and private citizens who actually live and work on the land. They are people like the citizens of Lemhi County, Idaho, who toil on the land every day of their lives and don't get their names in the newspapers. They don't get to testify in court. They don't send out fund-raising letters. They don't collect thousands of dollars in consultant fees. They don't get asked to serve as assistant secretaries of the Interior. They are as anonymous as the people who build your cars and televisions, who grow your food, and who drill for the oil to heat your home. But at the moment that photo was taken in Salmon, they weren't anonymous any longer. They were real people. People whose way of life was threatened by activists and bureaucrats who couldn't tell a salmon from a salesman.

Patti Burke, the social services director for Lemhi County, spoke for the citizens of Salmon:

I have been the welfare director of an isolated county in Idaho for the past five years. The Department of Health and Welfare has labeled our county as 'frontier.' We have our hardships from the isolation but we also enjoy clean air and beautiful mountains. My own family has lived in this Lemhi Valley since 1867 when they arrived by wagon train. Our roots and love for this area are very strong and our heritage has anchored us here. We have always believed that we are lucky to live here and are caretakers of the land. Some of

178

my ancestors mined, ranched, taught, and worked for the State Highway Department, and my grandfather, Howard Sims, served many terms as a state legislator. Through this ancestry the value of working hard and fighting for what is right has become ingrained in my everyday life.

There are days I fight for the rights of senior citizens, mentally ill, poor, disadvantaged, victims of domestic violence, the terminally ill and so on. The battle now is for an entire community held hostage by the federal court system. Once again, people that do not live here or have any idea of the culture, economy, and environment are threatening our lives and livelihoods.

Whether it was the photo or the letters or the local publicity (the major media wouldn't touch the story), the Forest Service coordination paperwork was hurried through within six weeks and Judge Ezra dissolved the court injunction on March 8, saving Salmon from extinction. The real stewards of the land gained a small victory over the armchair frontiersmen. Lemhi County residents won a reprieve. Next time, they might not be so lucky. The Fish and Wildlife Service is exploring the possibility of transplanting grizzly bears into the Selway-Bitterroot ecosystem. Biologists estimate that the area could sustain a new population of at least 200 grizzlies.

11

HOPE FOR THE FUTURE

"When neither their property nor their honor is touched, the majority of men live content."

—Niccolo Machiavelli

Unlike the members of the eco-federal coalition, the citizens of Lemhi County and their compatriots in the property rights movement do not want a self-perpetuating struggle. They have jobs, families, chores, and hobbies to occupy their time. The leaders of the property rights movement would like nothing more than to go back to their daily lives. But, as we all know, the price of freedom is eternal vigilance. So these citizens pull on their boots each morning and go out to fend off another attack against their constitutional rights.

It is a difficult struggle. If you win you end up keeping what you have. You are no further ahead. If the environmental activists lose a battle, their property is not taken away from them. They go on much as before. In fact, they use the property rights movement as a bogeyman to scare up more contributions for themselves. But the

180

tide will turn when the urban and suburban centers of our nation realize that this is their fight, too. Former Wyoming Senator Malcolm Wallop puts it into perspective: "If you possess a diamond necklace and somebody took a diamond out of it, you would surely expect to be compensated for that one diamond, even though you still possess the necklace . . . that's property and it begins to take on the same meaning in people's minds."

The struggle for property rights has taken on an unfortunate "East vs. West" flavor in recent years. A robust battle occurred in the Senate over a bill that would have designated 2 million acres of Utah as wilderness. Environmental groups wanted 5.7 million acres. "What I want to preserve is the possibility for silence and the possibility for time that exists only in the wilderness," said Senator Bill Bradley of New Jersey. "We know what silence and time is," responded Senator Orrin Hatch of Utah. It seems that many policy makers and opinion makers in Eastern states (or large urban areas) see in the West a past that has been lost in their areas. They have visions of empty prairies, tumbleweeds, and the mournful howls of coyotes. They see the traffic and bustle of their cities and long to preserve a place of silence.

Westerners understand that feeling. But the West is their *home*. When the government places unreasonable restrictions on hunting, fishing, farming, discing, and dozens of other activities, it is in essence ordering Westerners to live like Easterners. This is what causes friction. Imagine a national government with its capital in Salt Lake City telling the residents of New York and Washington that garbage Dumpsters and elevators are harmful to the environment—requiring them to take their own trash to the dump, and walk up stairs to get to their offices on the sixteenth floor. My guess is that Eastern representatives would tell those hypothetical federal bureaucrats to go jump in that Great Salt Lake.

Westerners are often accused of nostalgia for frontier days. But Easterners often use that same nostalgia to restrict open Western

181

spaces. People used to ride through the deserts of the Southwest on horses, but asking them to do it today, in the name of preserving the wilderness, is a hardship. This is particularly true when they need to carry pipe to fix a well. People used to regularly encounter bears, mountain lions, and wolves in the wilderness. Asking them to risk their lives today as they did one hundred years ago is asking a bit much. People back then put up with such things because they had to. Think of it this way: In the nineteenth century, people in the Northeast worked all summer in buildings with no air-conditioning. They sidestepped vast amounts of horse manure while walking through the streets. They had to shop for food every day because there was no refrigeration. They did all these things, but the suggestion that they should do so again today would be met with strong protest. This is how many Westerners react when told to accept the presence of predators or wetlands on their property.

Today's land battles are not about "use" versus "nonuse." Setting aside huge tracts of land for wilderness is a use. If this is done, it is supposed to mean that Americans, through their government representatives, have determined that *using* land for wilderness has more societal value than using it for something else. But is that what is happening today? When we make our choices between scenery and sewers are we doing so with all the facts in our possession, with rigorous science, with controlled emotion, with considered priorities, and with a strong adherence to the United States Constitution? And who best to make those choices? Are the people who give us slow mail service, low SAT scores, and the 1040 tax form best suited to control millions of acres of land? Enormous local effects call for decision making at the most local level possible.

The environmental movement will fight tooth and nail against this tendency toward governmental devolution. The centralization of political power in Washington, D.C. is the most crucial element to the continued influence of the big environmental groups. Efforts to restore a measure of federalism are meeting fierce resistance.

There are proposals in Congress to sell some marginal national parks to state or local governments or to private concerns. The sites would be selected by a commission similar to the one that recommended military base closures. Stop right there, say the defenders of the status quo. "It is part of a radical agenda that is anti-environment and pro-development and pro-state control," said Representative Bill Richardson (D-New Mexico) "Who is going to protect the national interest here? . . . Developers? Local mayors?"

Despite Representative Richardson's disdain, some local mayors are showing the way to a new philosophy of government. They are reducing the size of government, reducing regulations, and reducing taxes. Bureaucracies are being cut and privatization is on the rise. Mayors such as Stephen Goldsmith of Indianapolis, Indiana, and Richard Vinroot of Charlotte, North Carolina, say the principles that have worked for them can be applied to the federal government. Governors John Engler of Michigan and Tommy Thompson of Wisconsin are doing the same for state government. Their advice: Cut taxes and red tape. Concentrate on crime and infrastructure. Allow the private sector to do more. Treat taxpayers as customers. "There's a debate now about turning many of the services now performed by the federal government over to state and local government," says William Eggers of the Reason Foundation. "I think that the record shows that those lower levels of government can be trusted. In fact, most of the innovation in government that has occurred in the last twenty years has occurred at the state or local level." Such decentralization of political power means more empowerment to the people, just as the Founders intended. It would break the grip of the eco-federal coalition, who cannot win a fight in all fifty state legislatures and thousands of city halls. It would also end the disgust that people of all political stripes currently feel about government and the political process.

There is rare agreement among political thinkers about the tendency of governments to exceed their authority and bring about un-

intended consequences. The power of the state in the hands of people with an idealist agenda, that are also out of touch with reality,
frightens the average American. Liberals feel this is mostly true of
the military and intelligence establishments. Conservatives believe
it of those who develop the nation's social and environmental policies. There is a new program underway that may frighten both sides
equally. At the urging of Vice President Al Gore, U.S. intelligence
agencies are directing spy satellites to study "ecologically sensitive"
sites around the world. This new $15 million program will ultimately
monitor 500 sites in the United States and around the world.
MEDEA, which stands for Measurements of Earth Data for Environmental Analysis, is a group of sixty scientists who advise the nation's intelligence agencies on the use of secret data to study the
environment. They are conducting experiments to see how effectively these spy satellites can monitor natural sites. "Federal civilian
agencies" will nominate areas for monitoring. Some of the current
candidates are the Mojave Desert in California, the Konza prairie in
Kansas, and Fish Creek, Alaska.

"There are people who will paint this as soft-headed environmentalism," said Steven Aftergood, a senior researcher at the Federation of American Scientists. "But in fact environmental changes
can be an important source of regional conflict, so I think it's a perfectly legitimate redirection." I am not familiar with any discipline
of intelligence analysis that can predict the outbreak of armed conflicts by observing the vegetation. But such satellites are ideal for
monitoring human intrusion into ecologically sensitive areas. The
supporters of the Wildlands Project will finally find some technology they like. The supporters of centralized power will like it even
more.

The Founders designed our government with three independent
branches in order to establish a system of checks and balances. De-

spite complaints from holders of all sorts of political viewpoints, the branches have done an exceptionally good job of keeping each other in check. What has been wholly missing, particularly in this century, is any notion of *self-restraint* on the part of the individual branches. Judges rule that overflying geese are "commerce," presidents appoint environmental officials straight from the ranks of advocacy groups, and members of Congress introduce and pass bills that remove millions of acres from the tax rolls. Each branch of government would experience an immediate rise in public esteem if it only understood the phrase "Butt out." Politicians and officials who treat the Constitution as a document that limits *their own power* will find respect among America's citizens.

Skepticism of government activism is at an all-time high. Whether the national media is sufficiently skeptical of government is open to argument. What appears to be beyond argument is the press's tendency to accept environmental claims without skepticism. We have all seen the headlines: "Coming from Congress: Dirty Water, Foul Air" or "Species Disappearing at Record Rates." Headlines like these frighten politicians who want to loosen the grip of the eco-federal coalition. Republicans tend to score low on opinion polls about the environment. But when questions about constitutional protections of property are added, the numbers rebound. A poll conducted by the Competitive Enterprise Institute (CEI) in August 1995 showed that the American public supports much stronger Endangered Species Act reforms than have been proposed so far in Congress. "The current Endangered Species Act is a disaster for both people and wildlife," said Ike Sugg, CEI's fellow in land and wildlife policy. "This poll shows Congress lags far behind the public's support for real reform." According to the poll, only 11 percent of Americans support the current ESA, which regulates private land use without compensating landowners for their losses. Thirty-seven percent support compensation for "any loss" incurred by landowners as a result of the ESA's regulation of private property.

185

Thirty-five percent support the adoption of a nonregulatory, incentive-based approach to species conservation. "That 72 percent of those polled believe private landowners should not be made to suffer *any* uncompensated losses under the ESA is significant," said Sugg. "That 35 percent of them believe that even *compensated* takings are inferior to not regulating private property at all, is astounding."

Most of my legislative efforts have focused on the Endangered Species Act, though the principles apply to other environmental issues as well. As with most laws, the goals of the ESA are undeniably noble. However, it must be comprehensively rewritten to restore it to its original intent. The current ESA imposes stifling bureaucratic regulations to accomplish the goal of species conservation. This is no longer necessary in an era of new environmental awareness on the part of the American people. People want to save species and want incentives to do so—not conflict and controversy.

Conservation efforts should be based on the best possible science to restore the faith of the public in decisions made by its government. Listing decisions should be made on current, factual information and require an adequate peer review of all of the data. All of the data used in the listing process should be open to the public. Voluntary measures to protect species should be encouraged, including: cooperative management agreements, habitat reserve grants, land exchanges, and habitat conservation planning. This would represent a dramatic positive shift from the current law.

The current act imposes burdens on individual private landowners when biologically valuable resources are discovered on their property. Since it does not recognize constitutionally protected private property rights, the ESA gives landowners no incentive to harbor endangered species. Instead, it places the costs and the burden of species conservation not on society as a whole, but on the backs of private property owners.

The ESA should protect private property rights. It should recognize that the goal of species conservation is a societal benefit, therefore society should bear the costs. By punishing private property owners for having endangered species on their property, we have caused people to fear the Endangered Species Act, not embrace it.

The bill I introduced to reform the Endangered Species Act compensates private property owners when the restrictions imposed by this law diminish the value of their land by 20 percent or more. By recognizing private property rights, landowners will no longer fear having endangered species on their land. The result will be an unleashing of the conservation ethic within our nation's landowners—and the dramatic enhancement of our rich biological heritage.

Our efforts to save species should incorporate the innovative ideas emerging from the American people. Scientific advances in captive breeding and species propagation programs should be utilized to restore threatened or endangered species to greater numbers and return them to the wild. Advances in scientific technology should be welcomed and encouraged, not hindered with rigorous paperwork and senseless bureaucracy.

The current ESA has been driven not by biology, but instead by the courts and the manipulation of public participation provisions in the law. For example, the public process to petition a listing of a species requires little scientific data, yet it requires the Fish and Wildlife Service to extensively consider what little it is given. In addition, as the spotted owl fiasco makes clear, frivolous lawsuits have contributed not to the conservation of the species, but instead to the economic and social upheaval of our rural communities.

Public participation should be encouraged—but in a more positive, constructive manner than under current law. *All* scientific data should be made available to the public. People who petition to list a species should provide more thorough and concise scientific information for that species to be considered. Finally, states need to be more actively involved in endangered species conservation by giving them incentives to implement this program.

My bill establishes a National Biodiversity Reserve System consisting of more than 290 million acres of land for the purpose of protecting biodiversity and our natural resource heritage. A proactive program, the biodiversity reserve system will utilize conservation lands to foster biodiversity and conserve endangered species. Lands can be added to the system by exchanging properties with nonfederal landowners. This is a positive shift from the current conservation practices in these areas.

It represents a dramatic and fundamental reform of the existing law by recognizing that the key to protecting threatened or endangered species is through incentives and rewards, not threats and fines. Rewarding people for species conservation and good land stewardship is the key to strengthening the Endangered Species Act. It is that simple.

The current Endangered Species Act is being implemented without consideration of the social and economic impacts that listings create. In many cases, it is also not being implemented with common sense. We need to change the Endangered Species Act to provide— in law—a measure of certainty for communities and individuals. We also need to prevent the endangering of human lives to protect species.

The balance of wildlife protection has swung too far away from meeting the needs of the people of this country for food, clothing, housing, fuel, and other vital public goods and services. For those who are farmers and ranchers, their entire lives have been shaped by the traditions and values associated with the proper stewardship of the land. Yet they are considered to be the bad guys by government bureaucrats who think that only they know how to best protect endangered species.

Natural resources should be managed with sanity and reason. It is possible to find an equilibrium between conserving the land and meeting the needs and rights of people. We should replace regula-

tory nightmares with an incentive-based approach toward the protection of species. By providing incentives, and not threats, we will
find ways to conserve our biological resources without the heavy
hand of central bureaucracy.

No responsible person is opposed to protecting truly endangered
species. Their protection does provide a significant public benefit,
but the rights of property owners need not be sacrificed to protect
endangered species. This does not have to be an "either-or" debate.

The 104th Congress has begun the process of restoring private
property rights. While property owners are now getting a fair hearing in environmental debates, progress in the field has been painfully
slow. Environmental groups are screaming about a Republican Congress trying to set back the clock on clean air and water, but we still
have people like Tom Holloway of Beaver Lake, Arkansas, under the
federal gun.

The U.S. government filed charges against Holloway for the rep-
rehensible crime of "unauthorized modification of vegetation cover
on federal lands"—a misdemeanor that carries a penalty of up to six
months in prison and a fine of up to $500. In the spring of 1991, Hol-
loway's son was bitten by a copperhead snake while walking through
a 100-foot land corridor under the jurisdiction of the Army Corps
of Engineers. The corridor separates Holloway's property from his
boat dock. Holloway notified the corps that it needed to mow the
grass. When the corps took no action, Holloway mowed the corridor himself.

Unfortunately for Holloway, the corps has a regulation that bans
anyone from mowing grass more than fifty feet into corps property
without a written permit. Now Holloway faces a jail term because
he wanted to protect his family from snakes and the corps would not
cut its grass. What is worse, the government seems to feel that prosecuting Holloway is worth the taxpayers' time and expense. While
the corps has lost all sight of common sense, Holloway has a deeper

understanding of the issues involved. "It's a matter of greater en-croachment of the government into private property rights," he said. "It's about freedom."

People like Tom Holloway should not be treated like criminals. A bipartisan group of lawmakers has introduced a number of bills aimed at returning common sense to the relationship between landowners and government. HR 2275, The Endangered Species Conservation and Management Act of 1995, fundamentally reforms the Endangered Species Act by creating a balanced method of pro-tecting endangered species while still safeguarding the rights of pri-vate property owners and workers, meeting public safety and health needs, and achieving species conservation and recovery. First, it cleans it up the procedures for listing species by requiring scientific peer review before a species can be listed, avoiding any future "Mex-ican duck" listings. It encourages greater public participation in the process and limits the listing of "distinct population segments." Sec-ond, the act extends greater protection for property rights and of-fers incentives to protect threatened and endangered species. It compensates private property owners when restrictions imposed by the ESA diminishes their property's value by 20 percent or more. If ESA provisions devalue their property by 50 percent or more, the government would be required to buy it. Critical habitat could not be designated on private property without the permission or com-pensation of the owner. Third, and most important, it gives the states a greater role in implementation of ESA. The Secretary of the Inte-rior would have to consult with the states prior to listing decisions, critical habitat determinations, and issuances of final conservation plans.

Other bills include:

• HR 2284, The Conservation Habitat Reserve Program Act, would establish a new program to encourage owners of agri-cultural land to care for endangered or threatened species in exchange for cash payments. Contracts are to be for five to ten years. The land must be occupied by a protected species to receive payments.

- HR 2285, The Theodore Roosevelt Commemorative Coin Act, would provide a funding source for that program.
- HR 2286, The Endangered Species Conservation Incentives Act of 1995, would encourage landowners to enter into agreements to benefit endangered or threatened species by excluding land used for their protection from estate taxes. It would also provide an enhanced tax deduction for the donation of land for conservation purposes and a tax credit for the costs of complying with a conservation agreement.

Similar measures can be applied to preserve wetlands, deserts, and waterways. But many property rights violations cannot be solved legislatively or through the courts. When government agencies can regulate and seize property with no written authorization from the representatives of the people, that's tyranny. It will take a nationwide effort to demand that our government officials obey the laws set out by Congress and signed by the president *before* they demand compliance from the people. The examples I have cited in this book indicate that too many of our tax dollars go to government lawyers who go to court to argue that the terms "interstate commerce," "just compensation," and "navigable waters of the United States" mean something other than what they say. Americans should demand that our public servants understand and abide by the laws our Founders wrote.

We must expose the language of extreme environmentalism. Just as government tries to conceal its passion for taxes behind words and phrases like "user fees," "assessments," and "revenue enhancements," the eco-federal coalition and its minions in the media have their own set of words to hide their true agenda. "Sustainable development" really means "no growth," particularly of production agriculture or residential development. "Public lands" are in actuality lands held, controlled, and run in excruciating detail by the federal government—the landlord from hell. An "ecosystem" is any place with trees and/or animals. "Wetlands" are swamps or, as the Corps of Engineers official informed us, "anything we say it is." A mud puddle becomes a "vernal pool." "Balance of nature" means no humans. A "distinct population" means there are unendangered animals near a development site. A "conservancy" is a real estate firm.

The men who wrote the Constitution were not slick lawyers, bureaucrats, or semanticists. They were, however, property owners and tradesmen. Those of us who want to reform America's environmental laws believe the Founders would support our view. Assistant Interior Secretary George Frampton Jr. (former president of the Wilderness Society) called our efforts to reform the ESA "extreme measures." Many Americans feel that asking the federal government to abide by the provisions of the Fifth Amendment is not an "extreme measure." Justice Antonin Scalia, in his dissent from the *Sweet Home v. Babbitt* decision noted that extending wildlife protections to private lands "imposes unfairness to the point of financial ruin—not just upon the rich, but on the simplest farmer who finds his land conscripted to national zoological use." That kind of injustice is what is unacceptable to those who believe in American values.

We must not forget that the strength of this country is based not only on our natural environment, but also on the rich diversity of our people. The rights and privileges of owning a piece of property represent a major step toward the fulfillment of the American Dream. It is this dream that draws people of all races, creeds, and colors to our shores—such as my grandparents from Portugal. The continued pitting of property rights against environmental concerns serves only to do damage to them both. This issue requires a search for balance, and a solution that can produce win-win results.

Before such a balance can be achieved, government bureaucrats, environmentalists, and activist judges must hear one message. It is coming loud and clear from America's private property owners. It is a call for respect. It is the immovable starting point before any regulation of private property can commence. It is nonnegotiable. America's landowners are saying, with a determination that is characteristic of the American spirit: "This land is *our* land!"

Environmentalists are fond of telling us that we are "squandering our heritage" or "forsaking our birthright," and that the planet is on loan to us for future generations. But liberty is our true heritage. We received it from our ancestors and we pass it on to our children. America is both a land and a people. Neither should be sacrificed for the benefit of the other.

APPENDIX: THE U.S. CONSTITUTION

PREAMBLE

WE THE PEOPLE of the United States, in order to form a more perfect Union, establish justice, insure domestic tranquility, provide for the common defense, promote the general welfare, and secure the blessings of liberty to ourselves and our posterity, do ordain and establish this Constitution for the United States of America.

ARTICLE I

SECTION 1. All legislative powers herein granted shall be vested in a Congress of the United States, which shall consist of a Senate and House of Representatives.

SECTION 2. The House of Representatives shall be composed of members chosen every second year by the people of the several States, and the electors in each State shall have the qualifications requisite for electors of the most numerous branch of the State Legislature.

No person shall be a Representative who shall not have attained to the age of twenty-five years, and been seven years a citizen of the United States, and who shall not, when elected, be an inhabitant of that State in which he shall be chosen.

Representatives and direct taxes shall be apportioned among the several States which may be included within this Union, according to their respective numbers, which shall be determined by adding to the whole number of free persons, including those bound to service for a term of years, and excluding Indians not taxed, three-fifths of all other persons. The actual enumeration shall be made within three years after the first meeting of the Congress of the United States, and within every subsequent term of ten years, in such manner as they shall by law direct. The number of representatives shall not exceed one for every thirty thousand, but each State shall have at least one Representative; and until such enumeration shall be made, the State of New Hampshire shall be entitled to choose three, Massachusetts eight, Rhode Island and Providence Plantations one, Connecticut five, New York six, New Jersey four, Pennsylvania eight, Delaware one, Maryland six, Virginia ten, North Carolina five, South Carolina five, and Georgia three.

When vacancies happen in the representation from any State, the executive authority thereof shall issue writs of election to fill such vacancies.

The House of Representatives shall choose their Speaker and other officers; and shall have the sole power of impeachment.

SECTION 3. The Senate of the United States shall be composed of two Senators from each State, chosen by the legislature thereof, for six years and each Senator shall have one vote.

Immediately after they shall be assembled in consequence of the first election, they shall be divided as equally as may be into three classes. The seats of the Senators of the first class shall be vacated at the expiration of the second year, of the second class at the expiration of the fourth year, and of the third class at the expiration of the sixth year, so that one-third may be chosen every second year; and if vacancies happen by resignation, or otherwise, during the recess of the legislature of any State, the executive thereof may make temporary appointments until the next meeting of the legislature, which shall then fill such vacancies.

No person shall be a Senator who shall not have attained to the age of thirty years, and been nine years a citizen of the United States, and who shall not, when elected, be an inhabitant of that State for which he shall be chosen.

The Vice President of the United States shall be President of the Senate, but shall have no vote, unless they be equally divided.

The Senate shall choose their other officers, and also a President pro tempore, in the absence of the Vice President, or when he shall exercise the office of President of the United States.

The Senate shall have the sole power to try all impeachments. When sitting for that purpose, they shall be on oath or affirmation. When the President of the United States is tried, the Chief Justice shall preside: and no person shall be convicted without the concurrence of two thirds of the members present.

Judgment in cases of impeachment shall not extend further than to removal from office, and disqualification to hold and enjoy any office of honor, trust or profit under the United States: but the party convicted shall nevertheless be liable and subject to indictment, trial, judgment and punishment, according to law.

SECTION 4. The times, places and manner of holding elections for Senators and Representatives, shall be prescribed in each State by the legislature thereof; but the Congress may at any time by law make or alter such regulations, except as to the places of choosing Senators.

The Congress shall assemble at least once in every year, and such meeting shall be on the first Monday in December, unless they shall by law appoint a different day.

SECTION 5. Each House shall be the judge of the elections, returns and qualifications of its own members, and a majority of each shall constitute a quorum to do business; but a smaller number may adjourn from day to day, and may be authorized to compel the attendance of absent members, in such manner, and under such penalties as each House may provide.

Each House may determine the rules of its proceedings, punish its members for disorderly behaviour, and, with the concurrence of two-thirds, expel a member.

Each House shall keep a journal of its proceedings, and from time to time publish the same, excepting such parts as may in their judgment require secrecy; and the yeas and the nays of the members of either house on any question shall, at the desire of one-fifth of those present, be entered on the journal.

Neither House, during the session of Congress, shall, without the consent of the other, adjourn for more than three days, nor to any other place than that in which the two Houses shall be sitting.

SECTION 6. The Senators and Representatives shall receive a compensation for their services, to be ascertained by law, and paid out of the Treasury of the United States. They shall in all cases, except treason, felony and breach of the peace, be privileged from arrest during their attendance at the session of their respective Houses, and in going to and returning from the same; and for any speech or debate in either House, they shall not be questioned in any other place.

No Senator or Representative shall, during the time for which he was elected, be appointed to any civil office under the authority of the United States, which shall have been created, or the emoluments whereof shall have been increased during such time; and no person holding any office under the United States, shall be a member of either House during his continuance in office.

SECTION 7. All bills for raising revenue shall originate in the House of Representatives; but the Senate may propose or concur with amendments as on other bills.

Every bill which shall have passed the House of Representatives and the Senate, shall, before it becomes a law, be presented to the President of the United States; if he approves he shall sign it, but if not he shall return it, with his objections to that House in which it shall have originated, who shall enter the objections at large on their journal, and proceed to reconsider it. If after such reconsideration two thirds of that House shall agree to pass the bill, it shall be sent, together with the objections, to the other House, by which it shall likewise be re-considered, and if approved by two thirds of that House, it shall become a law. But in all such cases the votes of both Houses shall be determined by yeas and nays, and the names of the persons voting for and against the bill shall be entered on the journal of each House respectively. If any bill shall not be returned by the President within ten days (Sundays excepted) after it shall have been presented to him, the same shall be a law, in like manner as if he had signed it, unless the Congress by their adjournment prevent its return, in which case it shall not be a law.

Every order, resolution, or vote to which the concurrence of the Senate and House of Representatives may be necessary (except on a question of adjournment) shall be presented to the President of the United States; and before the same shall take effect, shall be approved by him, or being disapproved by him, shall be repassed by two thirds of the Senate and House of Representatives, according to the rules and limitations prescribed in the case of a bill.

SECTION 8. The Congress shall have power to lay and collect taxes, duties, imposts and excises, to pay the debts and provide for the common defense and general welfare of the United States; but all duties, imposts and excises shall be uniform throughout the United States;

To borrow money on the credit of the United States;

To regulate commerce with foreign nations, and among the several States, and with the Indian tribes;

To establish a uniform rule of naturalization, and uniform laws on the subject of bankruptcies throughout the United States;

To coin money, regulate the value thereof, and of foreign coin, and fix the standard of weights and measures;

To provide for the punishment of counterfeiting the securities and current coin of the United States;

To establish post offices and post roads;

To promote the progress of science and useful arts, by securing for limited times to authors and inventors the exclusive right to their respective writings and discoveries;

To constitute tribunals inferior to the Supreme Court;

To define and punish piracies and felonies committed on the high seas, and offenses against the law of nations;

To declare war, grant letters of marque and reprisal, and make rules concerning captures on land and water;

To raise and support armies, but no appropriation of money to that use shall be for a longer term than two years;

To provide and maintain a navy;

To make rules for the government and regulation of the land and naval forces;

To provide for calling forth the militia to execute the laws of the Union, suppress insurrections and repel invasions;

To provide for organizing, arming, and disciplining the militia, and for governing such part of them as may be employed in the service of the United States, reserving to the States respectively, the appointment of the officers, and the authority of training the militia according to the discipline prescribed by Congress;

To exercise exclusive legislation in all cases whatsoever, over such district (not exceeding ten miles square) as may, by cession of particular States, and the acceptance of Congress, become the seat of the Government of the United States, and to exercise like authority over all places purchased by the consent of the legislature of the State in which the same shall be, for the erection of forts, magazines, arsenals, dock-yards, and other needful buildings;—And

To make all laws which shall be necessary and proper for carrying into execution the foregoing powers, and all other powers vested by this Constitution in the Government of the United States, or in any department or officer thereof.

SECTION 9. The migration or importation of such persons as any of the States now existing shall think proper to admit, shall not be prohibited by the Congress prior to the year one thousand eight hundred and eight, but a tax or duty may be imposed on such importation, not exceeding ten dollars for each person.

The privilege of the writ of habeas corpus shall not be suspended, unless when in cases of rebellion or invasion the public safety may require it.

No bill of attainder or ex post facto law shall be passed.

No capitation, or other direct, tax shall be laid, unless in proportion to the census or enumeration herein before directed to be taken.

No tax or duty shall be laid on articles exported from any State.

No preference shall be given by any regulation of commerce or revenue to the ports of one State over those of another: nor shall vessels bound to, or from, one State, be obliged to enter, clear, or pay duties in another.

No money shall be drawn from the Treasury, but in consequence of appropriations made by law; and a regular statement and account of the receipts and expenditures of all public money shall be published from time to time.

No title of nobility shall be granted by the United States: And no person holding any office of profit or trust under them, shall, without the consent of the Congress, accept of any present, emolument, office, or title, of any kind whatever, from any King, Prince, or foreign State.

SECTION 10. No State shall enter into any treaty, alliance, or confederation; grant letters of marque and reprisal; coin money; emit bills of credit; make any thing but gold and silver coin a tender in payment of debts; pass any bill of attainder, ex post facto law, or law impairing the obligation of contracts, or grant any title of nobility.

No State shall, without the consent of the Congress, lay any imposts or duties on imports or exports, except what may be absolutely necessary for executing its inspection laws: and the net produce of all duties and imposts, laid by any state on imports or exports, shall be for the use of the Treasury of the United States; and all such laws shall be subject to the revision and control of the Congress.

No State shall, without the consent of Congress, lay any duty of tonnage, keep troops, or ships of war in time of peace, enter into any agreement or compact with another State, or with a foreign power, or engage in war, unless actually invaded, or in such imminent danger as will not admit of delay.

ARTICLE II

SECTION 1. The executive power shall be vested in a President of the United States of America. He shall hold his office during the term of four years, and together with the Vice President, chosen for the same term, be elected, as follows:

Each State, shall appoint, in such manner as the legislature thereof may direct, a number of electors, equal to the whole number of Senators and Representatives to which the State may be entitled in the Congress; but no Senator or Representative, or person holding an office of trust or profit under the United States, shall be appointed an elector.

The electors shall meet in their respective States, and vote by ballot for two persons, of whom one at least shall not be an inhabitant of the same State with themselves. And they shall make a list of all the persons voted for, and of the number of votes for each; which list they shall sign and certify, and transmit sealed to the seat of the Government of the United States, directed to the President of the Senate. The President of the Senate shall, in the presence of the Senate and House of Representatives, open all the certificates, and the votes shall then be counted. The person having the greatest number of votes shall be the President, if such number be a majority of the whole number of electors appointed; and if there be more than one who have such majority, and have an equal number of votes, then the House of Representatives shall immediately choose by ballot one of them for President; and if no persons have a majority, then from the five highest on the list the said House shall in like manner choose the President. But in choosing the President, the votes shall be taken by States, the representation from each State having one vote; a quorum for this purpose shall consist of a member or members from two-thirds of the States, and a majority of all the States shall be necessary to a choice. In every case, after the choice of the President, the person having the greatest number of votes of the electors shall be the Vice President. But if there should remain two or more who have equal votes, the Senate shall choose from them by ballot the Vice President.

The Congress may determine the time of choosing the electors, and the day on which they shall give their votes; which day shall be the same throughout the United States.

No person except a natural born citizen, or a citizen of the United States, at the time of the adoption of this Constitution, shall be eligible to the office of President; neither shall any person be eligible to that office who shall not have attained to the age of thirty-five years, and been fourteen years a resident within the United States.

In case of the removal of the President from office, or of his death, resignation, or inability to discharge the powers and duties of the said office, the same shall devolve on the Vice President, and the Congress may by law provide for the case of removal, death, resignation, or inability, both of the President and Vice President, declaring what officer shall then act as President, and such officer shall act accordingly, until the disability be removed, or a President be elected.

The President shall, at stated times, receive for his services, a compensation, which shall neither be increased nor diminished during the period for which he shall have been elected, and he shall not receive within that period any other emolument from the United States, or any of them.

Before he enter on the execution of his office, he shall take the following oath or affirmation:—"I do solemnly swear (or affirm) that I will faithfully execute the office of President of the United States, and will to the best of my ability, preserve, protect and defend the Constitution of the United States."

SECTION 2. The President shall be Commander in Chief of the Army and Navy of the United States, and of the militia of the several States, when called into the actual service of the United States; he may require the opinion, in writing, of the principal officer in each of the executive departments, upon any subject relating to the duties of their respective offices, and he shall have power to grant reprieves and pardons for offenses against the United States, except in cases of impeachment.

He shall have power, by and with the advice and consent of the Senate, to make treaties, provided two-thirds of the Senators present concur; and he shall nominate, and by and with the advice and consent of the Senate, shall appoint ambassadors, other public ministers and consuls, Judges of the Supreme Court, and all other officers of the United States, whose appointments are not herein otherwise provided for, and which shall be established by law: but the Congress may by law vest the appointment of such inferior officers, as they think proper, in the President alone, in the courts of law, or in the heads of departments.

The President shall have power to fill up all vacancies that may happen during the recess of the Senate, by granting commissions which shall expire at the end of their next session.

SECTION 3. He shall from time to time give to the Congress information of the State of the Union, and recommend to their consideration such measures as he shall judge necessary and expedient; he may, on extraordinary occasions, convene both Houses, or either of them, and in case of disagreement between them, with respect to the time of adjournment, he may adjourn them to such time as he shall think proper; he shall receive ambassadors and other public ministers; he shall take care that the laws be faithfully executed, and shall commission all the officers of the United States.

SECTION 4. The President, Vice President and all civil officers of the United States, shall be removed from office on impeachment for, and conviction of, treason, bribery, or other high crimes and misdemeanors.

ARTICLE III

SECTION 1. The judicial power of the United States, shall be vested in one Supreme Court and in such inferior courts as the Congress may from time to time ordain and establish. The judges, both of the Supreme and inferior Courts, shall hold their offices during good behaviour, and shall, at stated times, receive for their services, a compensation, which shall not be diminished during their continuance in office.

SECTION 2. The judicial power shall extend to all cases, in law and equity, arising under this Constitution, the laws of the United States, and treaties made, or which shall be made, under their authority;—to all cases affecting ambassadors, other public ministers and consuls;—to all cases of admiralty and maritime jurisdiction;—to controversies to which the United States shall be a party;—to controversies between two or more States;—between a State and citizens of another State;—between citizens of different States,—between citizens of the same State claiming lands under grants of different States, and between a State, or the citizens thereof, and foreign States, citizens or subjects.

In all cases affecting ambassadors, other public ministers and consuls, and those in which a State shall be a party, the Supreme Court shall have original jurisdiction. In all the other cases before mentioned, the Supreme Court shall have appellate jurisdiction, both as to law and fact, with such exceptions, and under such regulations as the Congress shall make.

The trial of all crimes, except in cases of impeachment, shall be by jury; and such trial shall be held in the State where the said crimes shall have been committed; but when not committed within any State, the trial shall be at such place or places as the Congress may by law have directed.

SECTION 3. Treason against the United States, shall consist only in levying war against them, or in adhering to their enemies, giving them aid and comfort. No person shall be convicted of treason unless on the testimony of two witnesses to the same overt act, or on confession in open court.

The Congress shall have power to declare the punishment of treason, but no attainder of treason shall work corruption of blood, or forfeiture except during the life of the person attainted.

ARTICLE IV

SECTION 1. Full faith and credit shall be given in each State to the public acts, records, and judicial proceedings of every other State. And the Congress may by general laws prescribe the manner in which such acts, records, and proceedings shall be proved, and the effect thereof.

SECTION 2. The citizens of each State shall be entitled to all privileges and immunities of citizens in the several States.

A person charged in any State with treason, felony, or other crime, who shall flee from justice, and be found in another State, shall on demand of the executive authority of the State from which he fled, be delivered up, to be removed to the State having jurisdiction of the crime.

No person held to service or labour in one State, under the laws thereof, escaping into another, shall, in consequence of any law or regulation therein, be discharged from such service or labour, but shall be delivered up on claim of the party to whom such service or labour may be due.

SECTION 3. New States may be admitted by the Congress into this Union; but no new State shall be formed or erected within the jurisdiction of any other State; nor any State be formed by the junction of two or more States, or parts of States, without the consent of the legislatures of the States concerned as well as of the Congress.

The Congress shall have power to dispose of and make all needful rules and regulations respecting the Territory or other property belonging to the United States; and nothing in this Constitution shall be so construed as to prejudice any claims of the United States, or of any particular State.

SECTION 4. The United States shall guarantee to every State in this Union a republican form of Government, and shall protect each of them against invasion; and on application of the legislature, or of the executive (when the legislature cannot be convened) against domestic violence.

ARTICLE V

The Congress, whenever two thirds of both Houses shall deem it necessary, shall propose amendments to this Constitution, or on the application of the legislatures of two thirds of the several States, shall call a convention for proposing amendments, which, in either case, shall be valid to all intents and purposes, as part of this Constitution, when ratified by the legislatures of three fourths of the several States, or by conventions in three fourths thereof, as the one or the other mode of ratification may be proposed by the Congress; provided that no amendment which may be made prior to the year one thousand eight hundred and eight shall in any manner affect the first and fourth clauses in the Ninth Section of the First Article; and that no State, without its consent, shall be deprived of its equal suffrage in the Senate.

ARTICLE VI

All debts contracted and engagements entered into, before the adoption of this Constitution, shall be as valid against the United States under this Constitution, as under the Confederation.

This Constitution, and the laws of the United States which shall be made in pursuance thereof; and all treaties made, or which shall be made, under the authority of the United States, shall be the supreme law of the land; and the judges in every State shall be bound thereby, any thing in the Constitution or laws of any State to the contrary notwithstanding.

The Senators and Representatives before mentioned, and the members of the several State legislatures, and all executive and judicial officers, both of the United States and of the several States, shall be bound by oath or affirmation, to support this Constitution; but no religious test shall ever be required as a qualification to any office or public trust under the United States.

ARTICLE VII

The ratification of the conventions of nine States shall be sufficient for the establishment of this Constitution between the States so ratifying the same.

Done in convention by the unanimous consent of the States present the seventeenth day of September in the year of our Lord one thousand seven hundred and eighty seven and of the independence of the United States of America the twelfth. In witness whereof we have hereunto subscribed our names,

Go. Washington, Presid't and deputy from Virginia
Attest William Jackson, Secretary
New Hampshire: John Langdon, Nicholas Gilman
Massachusetts: Nathaniel Gorham, Rufus King
Connecticut: Wm. Saml. Johnson, Roger Sherman

Appendix: The U.S. Constitution

New York: Alexander Hamilton

New Jersey: Wil. Livingston, Wm. Paterson, David Brearley, Jona. Dayton

Pennsylvania: B. Franklin, Thos. Fitzsimons, Thomas Mifflin, Jared Ingersoll, Robt. Morris, James Wilson, Geo. Clymer, Gouv. Morris

Delaware: Geo. Read, Richard Bassett, Gunning Bedford jun, Jaco. Broom, John Dickinson

Maryland: James McHenry, Danl. Carroll, Dan of St. Thos. Jenifer

Virginia: John Blair, James Madison Jr.

North Carolina: Wm. Blount, Hu. Williamson, Richd. Dobbs Spaight

South Carolina: J. Rutledge, Charles Pinkney, Charles Cotesworth Pinkney, Pierce Butler

Georgia: William Few, Abr. Baldwin

(The first ten amendments to the Constitution are called the Bill of Rights and were adopted in 1791.)

AMENDMENT I

Congress shall make no law respecting an establishment of religion, or prohibiting the free exercise thereof; or abridging the freedom of speech, or of the press; or the right of the people peaceably to assemble, and to petition the Government for a redress of grievances.

AMENDMENT II

A well regulated militia, being necessary to the security of a free State, the right of the people to keep and bear arms, shall not be infringed.

AMENDMENT III

No soldier shall, in time of peace be quartered in any house, without the consent of the owner, nor in time of war, but in a manner to be prescribed by law.

AMENDMENT IV

The right of the people to be secure in their persons, houses, papers, and effects, against unreasonable searches and seizures, shall not be violated, and no warrants shall issue, but upon probable cause, supported by oath or affirmation, and particularly describing the place to be searched, and the persons or things to be seized.

AMENDMENT V

No person shall be held to answer for a capital, or otherwise infamous crime, unless on a presentment or indictment of a Grand Jury, except in cases arising in the land or naval forces, or in the militia, when in actual service in time of war or public danger; nor shall any person be subject for the same offense to be twice put in jeopardy of life or limb; nor shall be compelled in any criminal case to be a witness against himself, nor be deprived of life, liberty, or property, without due process of law; nor shall private property be taken for public use, without just compensation.

AMENDMENT VI

In all criminal prosecutions, the accused shall enjoy the right to a speedy and public trial, by an impartial jury of the State and district wherein the crime shall have been committed, which district shall have been previously ascertained by law, and to be informed of the nature and cause of the accusation; to be confronted with the witnesses against him; to have compulsory process for obtaining witnesses in his favor, and to have the assistance of counsel for his defense.

AMENDMENT VII

In suits at common law, where the value in controversy shall exceed twenty dollars, the right of trial by jury shall be preserved, and no fact tried by a jury, shall be otherwise reexamined in any Court of the United States, than according to the rules of the common law.

AMENDMENT VIII

Excessive bail shall not be required, nor excessive fines imposed, nor cruel and unusual punishments inflicted.

AMENDMENT IX

The enumeration in the Constitution, of certain rights, shall not be construed to deny or disparage others retained by the people.

AMENDMENT X

The powers not delegated to the United States by the Constitution, nor prohibited by it to the States, are reserved to the States respectively, or to the people.

AMENDMENT XI

The judicial power of the United States shall not be construed to extend to any suit in law or equity, commenced or prosecuted against one of the United States by citizens of another State, or by citizens or subjects of any foreign State.

Appendix: The U.S. Constitution

AMENDMENT XII

The electors shall meet in their respective States, and vote by ballot for President and Vice President, one of whom, at least, shall not be an inhabitant of the same State with themselves; they shall name in their ballots the person voted for as President, and in distinct ballots the person voted for as Vice President, and they shall make distinct lists of all persons voted for as President, and of all persons voted for as Vice President, and of the number of votes for each, which lists they shall sign and certify, and transmit sealed to the seat of the government of the United States, directed to the President of the Senate;—The President of the Senate shall, in the presence of the Senate and House of Representatives, open all the certificates and the votes shall then be counted;—The person having the greatest number of votes for President, shall be the President, if such number be a majority of the whole number of electors appointed; and if no person have such majority, then from the persons having the highest numbers not exceeding three on the list of those voted for as President, the House of Representatives shall choose immediately, by ballot, the President. But in choosing the President, the votes shall be taken by States, the representation from each State having one vote; a quorum for this purpose shall consist of a member or members from two-thirds of the States, and a majority of all the States shall be necessary to a choice. And if the House of Representatives shall not choose a President whenever the right of choice shall devolve upon them, before the fourth day of March next following, then the Vice President shall act as President, as in the case of the death or other constitutional disability of the President.—The person having the greatest number of votes as Vice President, shall be the Vice President, if such number be a majority of the whole number of electors appointed, and if no person have a majority, then from the two highest numbers on the list, the Senate shall choose the Vice President; a quorum for the purpose shall consist of two-thirds of the whole number of Senators, and a majority of the whole number shall be necessary to a choice. But no person constitutionally ineligible to the office of President shall be eligible to that of Vice President of the United States.

AMENDMENT XIII

SECTION 1. Neither slavery nor involuntary servitude, except as a punishment for crime whereof the party shall have been duly convicted, shall exist within the United States, or any place subject to their jurisdiction.

SECTION 2. Congress shall have power to enforce this article by appropriate legislation.

AMENDMENT XIV

SECTION 1. All persons born or naturalized in the United States, and subject to the jurisdiction thereof, are citizens of the United States and of the State wherein they reside. No State shall make or enforce any law which shall abridge the privileges or immunities of citizens of the United States; nor shall any State deprive any person of life, liberty, or property, without due process of law; nor deny to any person within its jurisdiction the equal protection of the laws.

SECTION 2. Representatives shall be apportioned among the several States according to their respective numbers, counting the whole number of persons in each State, excluding Indians not taxed. But when the right to vote at any election for the choice of electors for President and Vice President of the United States, Representatives in Congress, the executive and judicial officers of a State, or the members of the legislature thereof, is denied to any of the male inhabitants of such State, being twenty-one years of age, and citizens of the United States, or in any way abridged, except for participation in rebellion, or other crime, the basis of representation therein shall be reduced in the proportion which the number of such male citizens shall bear to the whole number of male citizens twenty-one years of age in such State.

SECTION 3. No person shall be a Senator or Representative in Congress, or elector of President and Vice President, or hold any office, civil or military, under the United States, or under any State, who, having previously taken an oath, as a member of Congress, or as an officer of the United States, or as a member of any State legislature, or as an executive or judicial officer of any State, to support the Constitution of the United States, shall have engaged in insurrection or rebellion against the same, or given aid or comfort to the enemies thereof. But Congress may by a vote of two-thirds of each house, remove such disability.

SECTION 4. The validity of the public debt of the United States, authorized by law, including debts incurred for payment of pensions and bounties for services in suppressing insurrection or rebellion, shall not be questioned. But neither the United States nor any State shall assume or pay any debt or obligation incurred in aid of insurrection or rebellion against the United States, or any claim for the loss or emancipation of any slave; but all such debts, obligations and claims shall be held illegal and void.

SECTION 5. The Congress shall have power to enforce, by appropriate legislation, the provisions of this article.

AMENDMENT XV

SECTION 1. The right of citizens of the United States to vote shall not be denied or abridged by the United States or by any State on account of race, color, or previous condition of servitude.

SECTION 2. The Congress shall have power to enforce this article by appropriate legislation.

AMENDMENT XVI

The Congress shall have power to lay and collect taxes on incomes, from whatever source derived, without apportionment among the several States, and without regard to any census or enumeration.

AMENDMENT XVII

SECTION 1. The Senate of the United States shall be composed of two Senators from each State, elected by the people thereof, for six years; and each Senator shall have one vote. The electors in each State shall have the qualifications requisite for electors of the most numerous branch of the State legislatures.

SECTION 2. When vacancies happen in the representation of any State in the Senate, the executive authority of such State shall issue writs of election to fill such vacancies: Provided, That the legislature of any State may empower the executive thereof to make temporary appointments until the people fill the vacancies by election as the legislature may direct.

SECTION 3. This amendment shall not be so construed as to affect the election or term of any Senator chosen before it becomes valid as part of the Constitution.

AMENDMENT XVIII

SECTION 1. After one year from the ratification of this article the manufacture, sale, or transportation of intoxicating liquors within, the importation thereof into, or the exportation thereof from the United States and all territory subject to the jurisdiction thereof for beverage purposes is hereby prohibited.

SECTION 2. The Congress and the several States shall have concurrent power to enforce this article by appropriate legislation.

SECTION 3. This article shall be inoperative unless it shall have been ratified as an amendment to the Constitution by the legislatures of the several States, as provided in the Constitution, within seven years from the date of the submission hereof to the States by the Congress.

AMENDMENT XIX

SECTION 1. The right of citizens of the United States to vote shall not be denied or abridged by the United States or by any State on account of sex.

SECTION 2. Congress shall have power to enforce this article by appropriate legislation.

AMENDMENT XX

SECTION 1. The terms of the President and Vice President shall end at noon on the 20th day of January, and the terms of Senators and Representatives at noon on the 3d day of January, of the years in which such terms would have ended if this article had not been ratified; and the terms of their successors shall then begin.

SECTION 2. The Congress shall assemble at least once in every year, and such meeting shall begin at noon on the 3d day of January, unless they shall by law appoint a different day.

SECTION 3. If, at the time fixed for the beginning of the term of the President, the President elect shall have died, the Vice President elect shall become President. If a President shall not have been chosen before the time fixed for the beginning of his term, or if the President elect shall have failed to qualify, then the Vice President elect shall act as President until a President shall have qualified; and the Congress may by law provide for the case wherein neither a President elect nor a Vice President elect shall have qualified, declaring who shall then act as President, or the manner in which one who is to act shall be selected, and such person shall act accordingly until a President or Vice President shall have qualified.

SECTION 4. The Congress may by law provide for the case of the death of any of the persons from whom the House of Representatives may choose a President whenever the right of choice shall have devolved upon them, and for the case of the death of any of the persons from whom the Senate may choose a Vice President whenever the right of choice shall have devolved upon them.

SECTION 5. Sections 1 and 2 shall take effect on the 15th day of October following the ratification of this article.

SECTION 6. This article shall be inoperative unless it shall have been ratified as an amendment to the Constitution by the legislatures of three-fourths of the several States within seven years from the date of its submission.

AMENDMENT XXI

SECTION 1. The eighteenth article of amendment to the Constitution of the United States is hereby repealed.

SECTION 2. The transportation or importation into any State, Territory, or possession of the United States for delivery or use therein of intoxicating liquors, in violation of the laws thereof, is hereby prohibited.

SECTION 3. This article shall be inoperative unless it shall have been ratified as an amendment to the Constitution by conventions in the several States, as provided in the Constitution, within seven years from the date of the submission hereof to the States by the Congress.

AMENDMENT XXII

SECTION 1. No person shall be elected to the office of the President more than twice, and no person who has held the office of President, or acted as President, for more than two years of a term to which some other person was elected President shall be elected to the office of the President more than once. But this article shall not apply to any person holding the office of President when this article was proposed by the Congress, and shall not prevent any person who may be holding the office of President, or acting as President, during the term within which this article becomes operative from holding the office of President or acting as President during the remainder of such term.

SECTION 2. This article shall be inoperative unless it shall have been ratified as an amendment to the Constitution by the legislatures of three-fourths of the several States within seven years from the date of its submission to the States by the Congress.

AMENDMENT XXIII

SECTION 1. The District constituting the seat of Government of the United States shall appoint in such manner as the Congress may direct:

A number of electors of President and Vice President equal to the whole number of Senators and Representatives in Congress to which the District would be entitled if it were a State, but in no event more than the least populous State; they shall be in addition to those appointed by the States, but they shall be considered, for the purposes of the election of President and Vice President, to be electors appointed by a State; and they shall meet in the District and perform such duties as provided by the twelfth article of amendment.

SECTION 2. The Congress shall have power to enforce this article by appropriate legislation.

AMENDMENT XXIV

SECTION 1. The right of citizens of the United States to vote in any primary or other election for President or Vice President, for electors for President or Vice President, or for Senator or Representative in Congress, shall not be denied or abridged by the United States or any State by reason of failure to pay any poll tax or other tax.

SECTION 2. The Congress shall have power to enforce this article by appropriate legislation.

AMENDMENT XXV

SECTION 1. In case of the removal of the President from office or of his death or resignation, the Vice President shall become President.

SECTION 2. Whenever there is a vacancy in the office of the Vice President, the President shall nominate a Vice President who shall take office upon confirmation by a majority vote of both Houses of Congress.

SECTION 3. Whenever the President transmits to the President pro tempore of the Senate and the Speaker of the House of Representatives his written declaration that he is unable to discharge the powers and duties of his office, and until he transmits to them a written declaration to the contrary, such powers and duties shall be discharged by the Vice President as Acting President.

SECTION 4. Whenever the Vice President and a majority of either the principal officers of the executive departments or of such other body as Congress may by law provide, transmit to the President pro tempore of the Senate and the Speaker of the House of Representatives their written declaration that the President is unable to discharge the powers and duties of his office, the Vice President shall immediately assume the powers and duties of the office as Acting President.

Thereafter, when the President transmits to the President pro tempore of the Senate and the Speaker of the House of Representatives his written declaration that no inability exists, he shall resume the powers and duties of his office unless the Vice President and a majority of either the principal officers of the executive department or of such other body as Congress may by law provide, transmit within four days to the President pro tempore of the Senate and the Speaker of the House of Representatives their written declaration that the President is unable to discharge the powers and duties of his office. Thereupon Congress shall decide the issue, assembling within forty-eight hours for that purpose if not in session. If the Congress, within twenty-one days after receipt of the latter written declaration, or, if Congress is not in session, within twenty-one days after Congress is required to assemble, determines by two-thirds vote of both Houses that the President is unable to discharge the powers and duties of his office, the Vice President shall continue to discharge the same as Acting President; otherwise, the President shall resume the powers and duties of his office.

AMENDMENT XXVI

SECTION 1. The right of citizens of the United States who are eighteen years of age or older, to vote shall not be denied or abridged by the United States or by any State on account of age.

SECTION 2. The Congress shall have power to enforce this article by appropriate legislation.

AMENDMENT XXVII

No law varying the compensation for the services of the Senators and Representatives shall take effect until an election of Representatives shall have intervened.

INDEX

215

Index

Index

221

Pacific Legal Foundation, 92, 122*n*, 157, 160
Pacific Research Institute, 81
Pacific Rivers Council, 163, 164
Pelican History of the World, The (Roberts), 13, 16
Pendley, William Perry, 97, 140–141, 157, 160
People for the Ethical Treatment of Animals (PETA), 98
People for the West!, 156
Piazza, John, 58–59
Pierce, James L., 147–148
Pierce, Robert J., 55
Pilon, Roger, property rights and, 10–11, 29–30
Plato, 15
Political Economy Research Center (PERC), 157
Pollot, Mark, 174
Pombo family ranch, just compensation and, 113–115
Poore, Patricia, 126
Pope, Carl, 148–149
population control movement, environmentalists and, 110–111
Pozsgai, John, 69–70
preserves:
 forest, districts, 4
 Staten Island, 5
 urban, 4–5
 western, 80
 see also wildlife refuges
President's Council on Environmental Quality, 49
private property:
 ancient civilizations and, 14–16
 Catholic Church and, 13–14
 Commerce Clause of Constitution and, 26
 Constitution and, 5–6, 7, 20
 definition of, 8–9
 French Revolution and, 18
 government and, 21
 growth of state and taxation of, 17–18
 personal freedom and, 9, 190

and reform of ESA, 185, 186–187, 188
 see also property rights
Private Property Rights Roundtable, 71
property rights:
 abuses, 11, 155–156
 Americans with Disabilities Act and, 124–125
 Army Corps of Engineers and, 58–73
 Bible and, 12–13
 Bill of Rights and, 26–33, 115
 Catholic Church and, 14
 civil rights and, 6, 7, 10, 112
 Clean Water Act and, 58–77
 Congress and, 159–160, 189
 Constitution and, 21–33, 191
 definition of, 9–12
 East vs. West and, 181
 environmental concerns vs., 192
 environmentalists and, 96–112
 ESA and, 35
 Fifth Amendment to Constitution and, 5–6, 7, 20, 27–31, 113–115
 Founding Fathers and, 19, 21–22
 government and, 8–9, 190
 historic preservation vs., 116–121
 history of, 8–20
 importance of, 1–7
 individual, "greater common good" vs., 11
 individual freedom and, 11–12, 190
 James Madison on, 7, 21, 27–28
 John Locke and, 19
 Pombo family ranch and, 113–115
 prehistoric origins of, 12–14
 public, 78
 recycling laws and, 125–127
 scenic views and, 119–120
 supporters of, Taung Ming-Lin and, 43–46
 white pine laws and, 18–19
 zoning laws and, 120–124
 see also private property
Property Rights Foundation of America, 157–158

Index

Index